GLOBETROTTER™

Travel Guide

TURKEY

John Mandeville

NEW HOLLAND

★★★ Highly recommended
★★ Recommended
★ See if you can

Seventh edition published in 2013
by New Holland Publishers (UK) Ltd
London • Cape Town • Sydney • Auckland

10 9 8 7 6 5 4 3 2 1

website: www.newhollandpublishers.com

Garfield House, 86 Edgware Road
London W2 2EA, United Kingdom

Wembley Square, First Floor, Solan Road
Gardens, Cape Town 8001, South Africa

Unit 1, 66 Gibbes Street, Chatswood
NSW 2067, Australia

218 Lake Road, Northcote,
Auckland, New Zealand

Distributed in the USA by
The Globe Pequot Press, Connecticut

ISBN 978 1 78009 438 0

Keep us Current
Information in travel guides is apt to change, which is why we regularly update our guides. We'd be grateful to receive feedback if you've noted something we should include in our updates. If you have new information, please share it with us by writing to the Publishing Manager, Globetrotter, at the office nearest to you (addresses on this page). The most significant contribution to each new edition will receive a free copy of the updated guide.

Publishing Manager: Thea Grobbelaar
DTP Cartographic Manager: Genené Hart
Editors: Thea Grobbelaar, Carla Zietsman, Melany Porter, Claudia Dos Santos
Cartographers: Reneé Spocter, Luyolo Ndlotyeni, Tanja Spinola, Nicole Bannister, William Smuts, Éloïse Moss
Consultant: Melissa Shales
Picture Researchers: Shavonne Govender, Jan Croot
Design and DTP: Nicole Bannister, Éloïse Moss
Compiler: Elaine Fick
Reproduction by Hirt & Carter (Pty) Ltd, Cape Town
Printed and bound by Craft Print International Ltd, Singapore

Photographic Credits:
Chris Fairclough Colour Library: pages 26, 39, 60; **Michele Falzena/jonarnoldimages.com:** page 21; **LF/Dr R Cannon:** page 75; **LF/Juliet Highet:** page 57; **LF/Richard Powers:** pages 43, 90; **LF/Flora Torrance:** pages 74, 84; **LF/Terence Waeland:** page 30; **LF/Andrew Ward:** pages 35, 37, 38, 83; **Photobank/Adrian Baker:** pages 78, 86; **Photobank/Jeanetta Baker:** title page, 72, 81; **Photobank/Peter Baker:** pages 4, 12, 20, 22, 44, 73, 80; **Picture Bank Photo Library:** page 87; **Travel Pictures Ltd:** cover, pages 36, 69; **RHPL:** pages 29, 68; **RHPL/C Bowman:** page 114; **RHPL/Robert Frerck:** pages 13, 23, 24, 40, 42, 62, 65, 95, 98, 119; **RHPL/Lee Frost:** page 8; **RHPL/James Green:** page 14; **RHPL/Norma Joseph (F R G S):** page 6; **RHPL/Tim Megarr:** page 55; **RHPL/Michael Short:** pages 9, 27, 45, 104, 105; **RHPL/Adam Woolfitt:** pages 7, 11, 25, 28, 48, 51, 56, 66, 82, 93, 100, 106, 110, 113, 115, 116, 117; **Peter Ryan:** pages 15, 16, 17, 33, 50, 52, 54, 64, 71, 85, 97, 103, 108, 118.
[LF: Life File; RHPL: Robert Harding Picture Library]

Cover: *A carpet shop in Marmaris, Turkish Aegean.*
Title Page: *Thermal springs, Pamukkale.*

CONTENTS

1
Introducing Turkey

Few places rival Turkey as an East-West meeting point. This was the birthplace of the Greek civilization, the seat of the Ottoman Empire which spanned nearly 500 years and stretched from the Danube to the Persian Gulf. Modern Turkey has **historical sights** to match Europe's, first-class **resorts**, splendid beaches, winter and summer sports, trekking and mountaineering. Recently, the many religious shrines dedicated to the Christian, Islamic and Jewish faiths are enjoying a touristic revival.

Istanbul has a history stretching back over two millennia and a romantic setting second to none. The spectacular domes and minarets of the grand **mosques** dominate the skyline of the **Golden Horn**, while the **Topkapı Palace** guards the exquisite treasures of the Ottoman Empire.

Along the Aegean and Mediterranean coasts you can admire some of the finest classical ruins, including entire cities such as **Ephesus** and **Pergamon**. This coastline also has superb scenery. The barren heartland of Anatolia contains sites dating back to the mysterious Hittite era of the Bronze Age and the vast, incredible undergound cities and cave dwellings of **Cappadocia**. On the Black Sea coast, where Jason and the Argonauts sought the Golden Fleece, lies the legendary **Trabzon** (Trebizond), while eastern Turkey beckons with Lake Van and biblical sites such as **Mount Ararat**.

Turkey has a rich and varied cuisine. The teeming **bazaars** sell everything from junk to treasures. Good buys include carpets, kilims, jewellery and leather.

Top Attractions

*** **Topkapı Palace:** from here the sultans ruled.
*** **Cappadocia:** cave dwellings and underground cities.
*** **Blue Mosque and Aya Sofya:** Istanbul's most famous mosque and magnificent Byzantine church.
*** **Ephesus:** classical ruins in the eastern Mediterranean.
** **Nemrut Dağı:** carved heads on a remote mountain.
** **Sumela Monastery:** towering mountain fortress of the Byzantine Church.
** **Pergamon:** one of the ancient world's great cities.

◀ *Opposite: Ölüdeniz, one of the finest beaches in the Mediterranean region.*

Some Geographical Facts and Figures

Turkey's **landmass** is 779,452km² (300,868 sq miles). The **land border** totals 2753km (1711 miles).
Highest mountain: Mt Ararat (Agrı Dağı), an extinct volcano with a permanently snow-capped peak, which rises to about 5137m (16,853ft).
Largest lake: Lake Van, which covers an area of approximately 3738km² (1443 sq miles), and reaches a depth of about 100m (330ft).
Longest rivers: Two of the world's greatest rivers, the Tigris and the Euphrates, both rise in southeastern Turkey. The South East Anatolia Project (GAP), which harnesses the water power of these rivers, is Turkey's most ambitious hydroelectric scheme.
Population: Turkey has a population of approximately 78 million people.

THE LAND

Geographically Turkey forms part of a vast mountain range which arcs from the Balkans to Iran, characterized by sharp, steep peaks. The tectonic plates in this region are unstable, which results in numerous tremors, although serious **earthquakes** occur rarely. In 1999 one such earthquake struck an area centred on Izmit, with devastating results (*see* panel, opposite page).

The country is divided into seven regions: **Marmara**, the **Black Sea**, **Eastern Anatolia**, **Southeastern Anatolia**, the **Mediterranean**, the **Aegean** and **Central Anatolia**. There are over 80 administrative provinces. Although mountainous, Turkey has lush, fertile plains where cash crops (tobacco and cotton), fruit and vegetables (tomatoes, figs and apricots), nuts and cut flowers are produced. Heavy-handed state farming practices have seriously reduced yields. In the Kurdish areas of Eastern Anatolia, many people moved to cities to avoid sectarian clashes but the massive irrigation schemes of the GAP Project are producing a new generation of wealthy farmers.

Mountains and Plateaux

The average height above sea level of the Turkish landmass is approximately 1000m (3300ft) in the western part of the country, rising to some 2000m (6500ft) in the east. Over 90% of Turkey is mountainous, with most of the lower, flatter terrain along the coast.

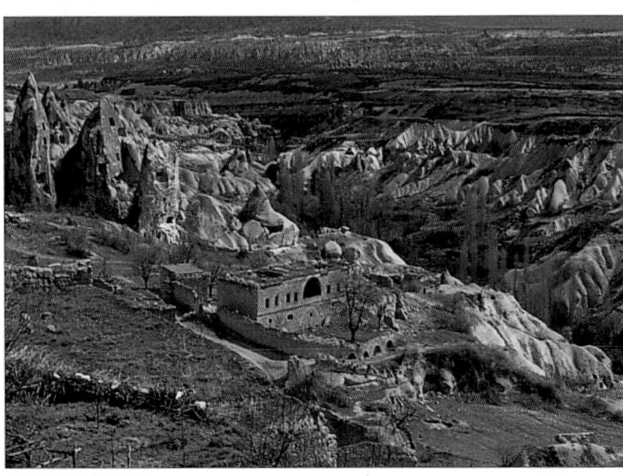

Forest-clad mountain ranges, rising to a height of over 3000m (10,000ft), run along the hinterland of the Black Sea and Mediterranean coasts. Inland between them lies the vast semi-arid Anatolian plateau. Much of this region is reminiscent of the Russian steppe with its lack of trees: a flat emptiness stretching towards immense horizons, spanned by huge skies, occasionally dotted with isolated settlements. The region has several large shallow salt lakes – most notably **Tuz Gölü** 130km (80 miles) to the south of Ankara – some of which can extend for almost 1500km² (600 sq miles). There are also several extinct volcanoes in this region. The most spectacular of these is **Erciyes Dağı**, which is permanently snow-capped and rises to almost 4000m (13,000ft).

▲ *Above: Eastern Turkey is a land of dramatic vistas, beautiful and forbidding.*
◀ *Opposite: Fairy Chimneys of Göreme in Cappadocia.*

The highest peak in Turkey is the imposing hulk of biblical **Mount Ararat**, an extinct volcano bordering Iran and Armenia. It is widely believed that Noah's Ark came to rest here after the Flood.

Rivers and Waterways

One of the most interesting geographical features of Turkey is the water link between the Black Sea and the Aegean. It is created by two narrow waterways formed from flooded river valleys: the **Bosphorus** and the **Dardanelles**, which link up with the landlocked **Sea of Marmara** in one of the world's busiest shipping lanes. The level of the Black Sea is higher than that of the Aegean, and is constantly being filled by several of the world's greatest rivers (including the Danube, the Volga and the Dnieper). As a result both the Bosphorus and the Dardanelles, which average less than 2km (1 mile) wide, have dangerous southerly currents.

Turkey stretches across the drainage basins of both the Indian and the Atlantic oceans, the divide running approximately north–south through the eastern part of the country. East of this, the rivers drain via the Caspian Sea and the Persian Gulf. To the west, they reach the ocean by way of the Black Sea, the Aegean and the Mediterranean.

7.4 On the Richter Scale

A killer earthquake, centred 100km (62 miles) east of Istanbul, struck the city's industrial rim bordering the Sea of Marmara on 17 August 1999. About 23,000 lives were lost and hundreds of thousands were left homeless. Many contractors skirted building and safety regulations. The State came in for some grim criticism for failure to act more prudently before and after the disaster. Three months later another major tremor, of similar magnitude, struck a less populous area between Ankara and Istanbul. There have been several quakes since, the last major one in October 2011 killing 600 people in Eastern Turkey.

Most notable among the rivers are the Büyük Menderes, Küçük Menderes and Gediz, which all flow into the Mediterranean; the **Seyhan** which flows into the Mediterranean south of Adana; and Turkey's longest river, the **Kızılırmak**, which courses along for approximately 800km (500 miles) before it flows into the Black Sea. The fabled **Tigris** and **Euphrates** rivers, which once cradled ancient Mesopotamia, both rise in eastern Turkey, before flowing into Iraq and Syria respectively. Both now support vast hydroelectric dam projects, creating huge artificial lakes, the water irrigating vast swathes of agricultural land in southeastern Turkey.

Seas and Shores

The rugged coastal region from the Dardanelles to Rhodes offers some of the finest scenery in the Aegean and is exceptionally well suited for **sailing**. Its main city, Izmir, is highly industrialized, but culturally more cosmopolitan than other urban centres. Around here are many lively resorts, such as **Kuşadası**, with fine beaches, lively nightlife, and many scenic attractions. This coastline also contains some superb classical sites, such as Ephesus, Pergamon and Assos. The Mediterranean coastal region is more jagged and less densely populated, and dotted with some popular, picturesque **resorts** including Kaş and Kalkan, plus **beaches** such as Ölüdeniz, Patara and Bodrum on the **Turquoise Coast**. Its main city, **Antalya**, is one of the prettiest in Turkey. The Black Sea coastal region to the north is delightfully green and often backed by rugged coastal mountains. Parts of this region are less dramatic than the Aegean and Mediterranean coasts while the lorries thundering through from Russia can mar the ambience of the relatively unspoiled resorts.

The coastline around the Sea of Marmara contains a few real gems, but is otherwise disappointing. Highlights are the **Marmara Islands**, which resemble those in the Aegean, and tend to attract mainly local tourists. The northern coast houses many industries which expanded from Istanbul's inner city to purpose-built industrial zones.

Trailing Across Turkey

The Lycian Way runs through the Toros Mountains and lowland coastal areas from Fethiye to Antalya. The St Paul's Trail begins in either Perge or Aspendos, east of Antalya, the two branches joining before heading northeast to Lake Egirdir. Both are roughly 500km (310 miles) long, have been professionally waymarked, and come with an accompanying website (www.lycianway.com) and guidebooks. The same organizers have also created a third route, the **Evliya Çelebi Way**, which runs from the Sea of Marmara (Hersek) to Iznik, Bursa, Kütahya, Afyonkarahısar and Uşak, in northwestern Turkey, and published a guide and maps to trekking in the Kaçkar Mountains of eastern Turkey.

Climate

Turkey has five main climatic regions. **European Turkey** and the coast around the Sea of Marmara enjoy a pleasant Mediterranean climate, tempered by cooler prevailing winds from the Black Sea. Winters tend to be moderate but wet, although Istanbul has at least one or two brief, but paralyzing, snowfalls each winter. Summers are warm but seldom oppressively hot.

The **Aegean** coastal region has long, hot summers, giving way to temperate winters with plenty of rain. Spring is a delight, with clear, crisp days and a gradual warming of temperatures.

The **Mediterranean** coastal region is officially classified as subtropical, and in summer it can become unbearably hot. The **Black Sea** coast is temperate and wet.

The Anatolian **hinterland** sees extremes of temperature: long, hot and dry summers, and freezing winters with heavy snowfalls. Rainfall decreases further to the east, the region close to the Syrian border being a virtual desert. In the mountains and to the east, temperatures also tend to extremes of hot and cold.

Bird Paradise

Kuşcenneti Bird Sanctuary lies beside Lake Kuş some 16km (10 miles) south of **Bandırma**, on the southern coast of the Sea of Marmara. Its name means 'bird paradise' and this is no exaggeration. The lake is on the main **migration routes** from Europe. Millions of birds pass through each year (well over 200 species have been spotted). The best time to visit the sanctuary is in October.

◀ Opposite: A secluded beach on the Turquoise Coast, balm to the eye.

▼ Below: Poppies bloom profusely in the central Anatolian springtime.

Plant Life

The coastal regions of Turkey are mostly covered with scruffy, sparse, Mediterranean-style vegetation.

The Aegean coast is famous for its **figs**, but it also has extensive **olive groves** and **vineyards**. Coniferous and deciduous **forests** cover some of the mountainsides up to a height of approximately 2000m (6500ft). During spring, barren hillsides are suddenly transformed into a mass of colour, covered by a breathtaking variety of blooms;

COMPARATIVE CLIMATE CHART	ISTANBUL				ANKARA				AEGEAN COAST			
	WIN	SPR	SUM	AUT	WIN	SPR	SUM	AUT	WIN	SPR	SUM	AUT
	JAN	APR	JULY	OCT	JAN	APR	JULY	OCT	JAN	APR	JULY	OCT
MAX TEMP. ºC	11	21	35	22	7	22	36	25	19	28	38	29
MIN TEMP. ºC	-4	1	11	3	5	0	10	6	4	3	21	16
MAX TEMP. ºF	52	70	96	72	45	72	97	78	67	82	101	85
MIN TEMP. ºF	25	34	52	38	22	32	50	43	39	38	70	62
RAINFALL mm	109	46	34	81	33	33	13	23	112	43	50	53
RAINFALL in	4	2	1	3	1	1	1	1	4	2	2	2

A Forgotten People Rediscovered

Until the early 20th century, the **Hittites** were an almost forgotten people. Practically nothing was known of them, apart from a few obscure references in the Bible and in ancient Egyptian records. In 1905, a German team excavating at **Boğazkale** discovered the remains of the capital of an ancient empire. Tablets covered with an unknown cuneiform script were unearthed; when these were deciphered, it was realized they represented the earliest example of Indo-European writing hitherto known.

Useful Words and Phrases

Yes/No • *Evet/Hayır*
Thank you • *Teşekkür ederim*
I do not understand you • *Anlamadım*
Do you speak English? • *Ingilizce biliyormusunuz?*
Yesterday • *Dün*
Today • *Bugün*
Tomorrow • *Yarın*
Good • *Iyi*
Bad • *Kötü*
Foreign exchange • *Kambiyo*
Foreign exchange • *Döviz para*
Inexpensive • *Ucuz*
Expensive • *Pahalı*
Very • *Çok*

it is impossible to exaggerate the magnificent beauty of this season.

The barren Anatolian hinterland experiences a similar metamorphosis in spring, with numerous kinds of **wild flowers**, from orchids to tulips, bursting forth from the seemingly arid terrain.

Wildlife

The more remote regions of Turkey are still today inhabited by animals which are now virtually extinct in the rest of Europe. Wild boars, hyenas and wolves are found, as well as the occasional bear. More common though, are flocks of **mountain goats**, and occasional glimpses of gazelles, deer and buffalo. Hunting is permitted in season.

The country is particularly rich in **bird life**. Turkey is on the main migration routes from Europe to Africa via the Middle East and birds of passage include swallows, storks and geese. Unfortunately, this also has its downside, as witnessed by the outbreak of bird flu in central Turkey early in 2006.

The Black Sea coast is renowned for its **tuna**, which circle this sea in shoals, thus providing intermittent but plentiful catches for local fishermen. Generally, however, the fish population in the coastal areas is dwindling fast. The southern and western coasts sustain a variety of Mediterranean fish, as well as **eels**, **octopus** and **squid**, while some rivers are stocked with **trout** and **carp**. Unfortunately the number of **dolphins** is rapidly decreasing.

Many species of **snake** inhabit the mountainous hinterland of Turkey. Almost all species of snakes in the country are poisonous. In arid regions, keep a watchful eye out for scorpions.

Mosquitoes and many other flying **insects** inhabit the flat flood plains. Despite the spraying of insecticide, mosquitoes remain something of a menace around the more popular tourist spots on the south coast. They seem resistant to many of the familiar insect repellants.

HISTORY IN BRIEF

▲ *Above: Temple ruins at Boğazkale, once the great city of Hattuşaş.*

Archaeological evidence suggests that Anatolia has been inhabited for many thousands of years. At Goblekitepe, near Sanlıurfa in southeastern Turkey, is the world's oldest known temple, dating back to 9500BC at the cusp of the period when hunter-gatherers were just beginning to domesticate dogs for hunting. The world's oldest domesticated grains, dating to the same period, have been found nearby in Urfa, while **Çatal Höyük**, south of Konya, is currently thought to be the world's second oldest town (after Jericho), with a population of around 5000 by the 7th millenium BC. No less than 13 levels have been excavated here. Among the many intriguing finds are the chubby, small fertility goddesses which can now be seen in the Ankara Museum of Anatolian Civilizations.

The Hittite Empire

At around 2000BC the people we now know as the **Hittites** arrived, almost certainly from the other side of the Caucasus. They established the first great empire in Anatolia, with their capital at **Hattuşaş** (now Boğazkale – *see* panel, opposite page). Fascinating remnants of this once great city can still be seen scattered over a wide area.

By the 15th century BC, the Hittites had conquered **Babylon** and had even begun to rival mighty **Egypt**. The inevitable happened, and these two great empires clashed in 1275BC. The victorious Egyptians recorded the battle on the walls of the Temple of Amun at Karnak in Egypt.

Ionia

The Hittite Empire declined in the 13th century BC. This coincides with the arrival in Anatolia of a mysterious race known as the Sea People, who probably came from islands in the Aegean and may have been of Phoenician descent. By this time several kingdoms had grown up along the Anatolian shores of the Aegean. One of these was **Troy**, and it's now thought that the Trojan War

The Gordian Knot

The small town of Gordion, 100km (65 miles) southwest of Ankara, was originally the capital of Phrygia, an early Greek kingdom. The town was named after its greatest king, Gordios. According to legend, a peasant named Midas fulfilled an oracle's prediction that the first man to enter the city gates would become its new king, since **King Gordios** had no heirs. In gratitude, Midas pledged a chariot to the deities, tying shaft and yoke with a mighty knot. It was said that whoever succeeded in untying it would become ruler of Asia. **Alexander the Great** arrived here in 334BC on his campaign of conquest, and it was he who solved the problem, by simply slicing the knot in two with his sword. Whether or not this was the intended solution, Alexander certainly went on to fulfil the predicted destiny.

▲ *Above: Ancient greats such as Thales and Hippodamus once walked through the gateway of the theatre at Miletus.*
▶ *Opposite: Arycanda's ancient theatre dates back to the 5th century BC.*

(1250BC) had little to do with Helen's abduction. It is far more likely that this was a war for control of the trade route through the nearby Dardanelles to the Black Sea. After the fall of Troy, **Greek colonies** began to spread all along the Aegean and Mediterranean coasts of Anatolia, founding colonies like Lydia, Lycia, Pamphylia and Cilicia.

The Aegean coastal region of Anatolia became known as Ionia, and is today generally recognized as the cradle of the Greek civilization. Cities in this region grew rich, establishing maritime trade links as far afield as Egypt and the south of France. In the 6th century BC the city of Miletus produced Thales, who is regarded as the first philosopher. Another citizen of Miletus, the architect Hippodamus, introduced the first grid plan, after a war with the Persians had virtually annihilated the city. The foundations for Western civilization were being laid. Within two centuries, many new forms of knowledge – such as geometry, physics, and biology – came into being. Today the ruins of Miletus are obscure. The coastline has shifted and buried the remains, leaving only the theatre, ruined baths and market places, surrounded by the marshlands of the Büyük Menderes flood plain.

Other Ionian cities and their rulers retain legendary status. **King Midas** was renowned for his wealth, according to myth all he touched turned to gold. Richer still was **King Croesus** of Lydia, whose capital was at Sardis (modern Sardes). Croesus and his subjects possessed so much gold that they needed a handy method for distributing it – and invented coinage. King Mausolus of **Halicarnassos** (today's Bodrum), was more concerned with the next life, and built himself a huge tomb which became one of the Seven Wonders of the Ancient World.

From the middle of the 6th century BC, the fragile network of Ionian city states faced a new threat. The huge Persian army overran Anatolia, but never managed to conquer Greece, where the civilization, which had grown up in Ionia, continued to flourish and develop.

The Coming of Islam

The prophet Mohammed was born in Mecca around AD570. The religion he founded was to galvanize the Arabs, and in the 7th century they invaded Anatolia, even reaching the shores of the Bosphorus. But they soon withdrew, consolidating their conquests throughout the Middle East and North Africa. As the Arabs departed from Anatolia, they made contact with a Turkoman tribe called the Seljuks, who adopted the Muslim religion. These were the first true Turks to establish themselves in Anatolia.

Two centuries later Anatolia was conquered by a Macedonian Greek army under the command of **Alexander the Great**. When, in 323BC, Alexander died unexpectedly, Anatolia fragmented into a number of separate states as his generals struggled for power.

The Roman Era

At the end of the 2nd century BC the Roman Empire gradually expanded into Anatolia. In 133BC the king of Pergamon left his kingdom to Rome; within a century, the entire Anatolian peninsula had been incorporated. They named this new territory **Asia Minor**. (Asia, or Asia Major, referred only to the Ionian region and the immediate hinterland.)

But Asia Minor proved a troublesome spot and was shaken by several rebellions. In 74BC Mithradates Eupator, notorious King of Pontus, the kingdom bordering the Black Sea, rose and slaughtered a large proportion of the Romans who had settled along the Ionian coast. Not until **Julius Caesar** arrived on the scene did he meet his match. Julius Caesar was back a quarter of a century later as emperor, to put down another rebellion in the Pontus. This time his army crushed Mithradates Eupator's son. It was during this campaign that he coined his famous motto: *Veni, vidi, vici* ('I came, I saw, I conquered').

During the 1st century AD, **Christianity** began to spread through the coastal cities of south and west Anatolia. St Luke is thought to have brought the aged **Virgin Mary** to live in Ephesus, while **Sts Peter**, **Paul** and **Barnabas** formally founded the Christian church in Antakya (Antioch) and Paul preached throughout Asia Minor.

Three centuries later the emperor himself was a Christian, but the empire had by this time begun to crumble and Emperor Constantine moved its capital east, from Rome to Byzantium (modern Istanbul).

Barbarossa

The pirate-admiral who ruled the Mediterranean for the Ottoman Empire, Barbarossa ('red beard'), was born towards the end of the 15th century on the Aegean island of Lesbos. His original name was Khayr al-Din and his mother was almost certainly Greek. He and his older brother, Arouj, established themselves as pirates, terrorizing the Barbary Coast (North Africa). They were so successful that they attempted to set up a kingdom here for themselves. When the Spanish attacked, Barbarossa sought help from the Turks and as a result Algeria and Tunisia became part of the Ottoman Empire. As reward for this acquisition, Barbarossa was made high admiral of the Turkish fleet and ruled the Mediterranean, devoting his life to ferocious attacks on Christian ships and coastal towns, striking fear wherever his vessels appeared.

Emperor Constantine

Constantine was born in the Balkans around AD280 and grew up at the court of the Emperor Diocletian. During the civil wars that racked the Roman Empire at that time, he led several armies, eventually taking over as emperor. Originally a worshipper of the sun, he later attributed his success to Christianity, having been spectacularly converted when he saw a shining cross in the sky. Although deeply religious, his theology was shaky, and as a result his Christianity retained certain elements of sun-worship. His first monuments and the coins of his new eastern capital bore solar symbols as well as the Christian cross.

Byzantium

Although Byzantium was renamed Constantinople and a new mega-city was built, the surrounding domain came to be known as the Byzantine Empire. When, during the 5th century, Rome was overrun by the Visigoths, the Byzantine Empire was all that remained of former glory days, as Europe descended into the Dark Ages.

The middle of the following century constituted a high point in the Byzantine Empire. The **Emperor Justinian** built the magnificent **Aya Sofya** in Constantinople around AD535. It was to remain the greatest church the world had ever seen for almost 800 years.

This empire was to suffer many vicissitudes, however, with threats coming from both east and west. Its most serious setback occurred at the hands of the **Crusaders**, who sacked Constantinople in 1204.

Meanwhile a new people had started to venture into eastern Anatolia. These were the **Seljuk Turks**, a Tartar tribe of Turkoman origin from central Asia, who had adopted the Muslim religion. They conquered half of Anatolia, leaving the **Ottomans**, who came after them to complete the task. In 1453, Sultan Mehmet II (the Conqueror) finally took Constantinople, banning the customary lootings and destruction of its buildings and renaming the city **Istanbul**.

▶ Opposite: A portrait of Sultan Mehmet II, conqueror of Byzantium.
▼ Below: The Aya Sofya, an architectural wonder built in the 6th century.

The Ottoman Empire

By the reign of **Süleyman the Magnificent** in the 16th century, the powerful Ottoman Empire covered most of North Africa and stretched as far west into Europe as the gates of Vienna, while extending east as far as the Yemen and the Persian Gulf. The Turkish fleet, under Barbarossa, ruled the Mediterranean.

On the whole, this was no vicious crushing empire. Ottoman rule was relatively easy-going in most instances and subjects were left to go about their business apart from the collection of taxes and occasional recruitment into the Turkish army. Members of the so-called **Janissary Corps**, the scourge of Europe, were initially forcibly recruited exclusively from among the sons of the Christian population of captured provinces. These recruits were converted to Islam, and originally celibacy was enforced – which turned out to be a sure-fire method of inducing ferocity.

Despite its generally lax attitude the Ottoman Empire brooked no internal rebellion, and any incipient local uprisings were quelled ruthlessly by the Janissaries.

Nevertheless, by the end of the 17th century the Ottoman Empire had begun an inexorable decline and the court of the sultan became notorious for its nasty intrigues and degenerate rule. The collapse of the Ottoman state was imminent.

By the 19th century, Turkey was generally regarded as **'the Sick Man of Europe'**, and started to attract the attentions of expansionist European powers (Russians, Austro–Hungarians, British, French and Germans). In the early 19th century, Ottoman territories in Greece, Bulgaria and Egypt had achieved their independence, and in the 1850s, the Crimean War erupted, partially due to Russian expansionist aims. The Turkish loss of the **Balkans** led to the chaotic Balkan Wars (1912–13) – a prelude to World War I.

The Fragmentation of the Balkans

The decline of the Ottoman Empire led to a volatile political situation in the Balkans. By the early 20th century a few small, independent, but fundamentally unstable states had emerged. Serbia, Albania, and Montenegro were soon embroiled in wars with their Balkan neighbours, often with three sides emerging. This contributed directly to World War I. The Balkans again showed their fragile nationalistic roots in the 1990s during the breakup of Yugoslavia and the Serb domination of Kosovo (the site of two key battles in 1389 and 1448 which led to Serbia being annexed to the Ottoman Empire). As NATO bombed the Serbs, hundreds of thousands of refugees streamed into neighbouring countries, including Turkey, while Turkish troops, arriving as peacekeepers in 1999, were hailed as saviours. How times change.

World War I

Paranoid about being annexed by Russia, Turkey sided with the Axis, Germany, Austria and Hungary, in the World War I, mistakenly believing she could stem the tide of disintegration. In spite of a brilliant campaign, led by **Mustafa Kemal**, which won Turkey its only victory at **Gallipoli** in 1915, Turkey lost not only the war but an empire.

Historical Calendar

c6400BC Human settlements at Çatal Höyük.
2000 Hittites arrive in central Anatolia.
1300 Collapse of Hittite Empire.
1250 Trojan War; Greek colonization.
550 Persian King Cyrus invades Anatolia.
334 Alexander the Great conquers Anatolia.
250 Great era of Pergamon.
130 Anatolia becomes a Roman province.
c50 St Paul preaches Christianity.
AD324 Emperor Constantine moves capital of the Roman Empire from Rome to Byzantium.
c550 Emperor Justinian constructs Aya Sofya.
c1050 Invasion of Seljuk Turks from Persia.
1204 Constantinople sacked by Crusaders.
1453 End of Byzantine Empire.
c1540 Height of Ottoman Empire.
1683 Turkish siege of Vienna.
1830 Greece independent of Ottoman rule.
1912 Start of Balkan War.
1914 World War I, Turkey joins German allies.
1915 Gallipoli Campaign.
1919 Mustafa Kemal (later Atatürk) leads War of Independence.
1922 Atatürk takes control of Turkey.
1939–45 World War II, Turkey remains neutral.
1952 Turkey joins NATO.
1960–80 During political instability, there are three military coups in 1960, 71 and 80, with the army restoring order then handing back power.
1988–2000 Kurdish separatists, the PKK conduct terror campaign in southeast Turkey.
2003 The AK religious party in government refuses to aid US in war on Iraq.
Nov 2003 Istanbul ripped by al-Qaeda bombs, aimed at synagogues and the British.
2004 onwards Kurdish separists resume armed struggle; to date the conflict has left 40,000 dead (mainly Kurds) and cost Turkey around US$300 billion.
2006 Initial talks on EU membership stall.
2010 Istanbul is European City of Culture.
2012–13 Turkey faces influx of Syrian refugees and military threat on its southern border.

The Allies, determined to carve up Turkey into strategic shares, gave very little thought to a national resistance movement in which Kemal's army would drive out the invading Greeks in 1920–23. Understandably, Kemal was not only a military hero but a saviour. He proclaimed himself head of the new republic and Father of the Turks, **Atatürk**. His glory and charisma continue to this day, in almost every town square, which has a statue of him.

Atatürk's **modernization** programme was initiated to make Turkey into a modern European state. Ottoman symbols, like the *fez* (a brimless hat adorned with a black tassel) and the veil for women were abolished. The capital of Turkey was moved from Istanbul to **Ankara**, where a thriving city was built out of a muddy village.

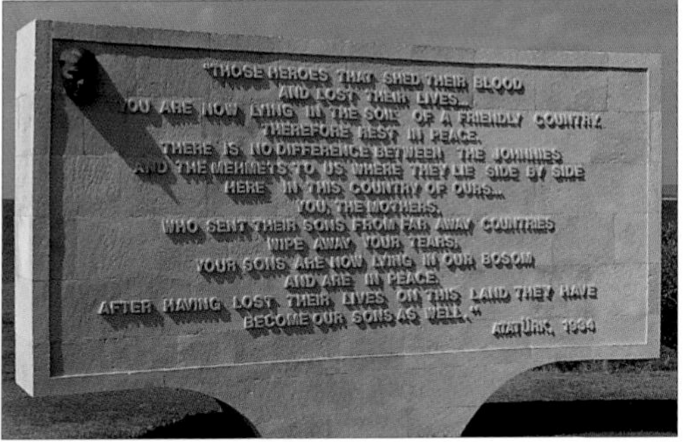

◀ *Left: After World War I, Atatürk erected a memorial to all those who lost their lives at Gallipoli.*
◀◀ *Opposite: A Turkish army veteran who served under Atatürk.*

Turkey after World War II

Turkey remained officially neutral during World War II but, nevertheless, gave enormous covert support to the Allies. The post-war era was marred by high unemployment, lack of funds to restructure and, subsequently, unrest was rife. Subconsciously, Turkey still feared Russia and leftist leanings or writings were political crimes. Muslim resistance to secular reforms also became more vocal. Turkey suffered three military coups between 1960 and 1980. The Kurdish population began increasingly to agitate for independence during this time. Many provinces lived permanently under military rule, including some sections of Istanbul.

Turkey from 1960 to the Present

Apart from Atatürk, another visionary helped to shape modern Turkey. **Turgut Özal** was Prime Minister in the 1980s and then became President until his death in 1993. Under Özal in the 1980s Turkey peeped out of its shell for the first time since World War I and began to emerge as an industrial economy and to export items. For a Turkey that had relied on government sponsored industries for basic needs, the prospect of exporting was exciting and the Özal era is remembered as dynamic and prosperous.

In 1996, the Refah (Religious Welfare) Party under Necmettin Erbakan was voted into power, largely on populist promises. Ousted by Turkey's generals in 1997, it was reformed as the Virtue Party then as the

Atatürk's Reforms

Atatürk's reforms of the 1920s and 1930s were radical in concept at the time. Imagine replacing the entire Arabic script with the western alphabet and expecting the population to learn to speak, read and write it virtually overnight! The Turkish alphabet is the same as the western one with a few resonance modifications. Reform of the educational and legal systems followed. Turkish women were given the right to vote and take office before women of many other countries. Polygamy was abolished and, most significant of all, Islamic rule was supplanted by a secular constitution, based broadly on Swiss laws. Not all favoured these reforms, particularly Kurds who had lost their claim to a part of Turkey granted by the Allies. Today, provocative clashes involving secular and sacred issues are frequently on political agendas.

AK (Justice and Development) Party, under leader Recep Erdoğan, which eventually took office in 2002, after promising to respect Turkey's secular constitution.

GOVERNMENT AND ECONOMY

The Constitution

Turkey is a republic governed by a national assembly with 550 members elected by ballot for five years. The 1924 constitution was replaced by a new one in 1961, introducing a parliament comprising a national assembly and a senate. Following a referendum in 1982, a new parliamentary system vested legal power in the Turkish Grand National Assembly and did away with the senate.

The **president** of the republic is elected for a seven-year term by the national assembly from members who are over 40 years of age and university educated. The day to day running of the country falls to the **prime minister** who is appointed by the president from among members of the national assembly. Ministers are then selected by the prime minister for various ministerial posts. In the event of a no-confidence vote on any issues, both the prime minister and the cabinet must step down.

Politics

Until 1946, Turkey had a single-party system but has since adopted a multi-party democratic system with elected parliamentary deputies. As a result, there are now over 60 political parties, although only a fraction of them are represented in parliament. For many years, no single party received a majority vote and there was a scramble to find suitable coalition partners. Parties whose aims were diametrically opposed to each other tried to adopt a working liaison but were often unsuccessful.

The AK Party took the parliamentary majority in 2002, but leader, Recep Erdoğan, had to wait until 2003 to win a by-election and become Prime Minister. The current President, Abdullah Gul, took office in August 2007 amidst great controversy. Formerly the Foreign Minister, his Islamist background alarmed secularists who did their best to block his appointment, holding vast political rallies

Turkish Biodata

- Turkey has a young population, with about 26.9% of people under 15 years old. Population growth rate has dropped very slightly in recent years to 1.2%. Numbers are evenly divided between the sexes.
- Around 70–75% of the population is Turkish, some 18% are Kurds, with the rest belonging to other minorities. The vast majority are Muslim (99.8%, most of them Sunni); the other 0.2% are mainly Christians and Jews.
- The literacy rate is high and getting higher, with 95.3% of men and 79.6% of women over the age of 15 able to read and write.
- Poverty is still an issue, with 16.9% of the population below the poverty line, 12% unemployment and 4% underemployment. Although Turkey's economy did shrink in the immediate aftermath of the 2008 global financial crisis, it bounced back spectacularly, achieving 8.5% growth in GDP in 2011. Inflation remains relatively high, but stable at around 6.5%.

Local Government

Turkey is divided into 81 provinces, each of which is overseen by a governor who represents the central government. Local government consists of elected councils and mayors. These usually stand as representatives of the main political parties.

and forcing a general election before he was confirmed. In 2008, the AK Party government was prosecuted for introducing an Islamist agenda, but escaped with a small fine. In 2010, they introduced a series of constitutional reforms to try and curb the strongly secular judiciary and military and relax the ban on headscarves, amongst a number of measures for greater gender equality and human rights. Some measures were immediately annulled by the courts; others were sent to a public referendum. Meantime, Turkey's military are never far from the political scene and the clash has led recently to a massive headline trial of some 350 high-ranking members of the military, judiciary and press charged with conspiring to overthrow the government.

▲ *Above: The Turkish flag.*

Politics is serious stuff in Turkey. Voting is by secret ballot but everybody knows everybody's political identity, and political cronyism and patronage are a way of life.

The Judiciary

Turkish judges have very wide powers of authority. Without a jury system, the judge alone decides on a case. The system does not assume innocence until guilt is proven. In minor cases, guilt is often apportioned with no one party being 100% innocent or guilty.

The independence of the judicial system is frequently under severe strain. Judges carry a huge case load and with a system that has no juries, also carry a heavy responsibility. The constitution is one of the most egalitarian and forward-thinking in the world but law, in practice, has not always followed it in spirit. However, things are changing; the death penalty was dropped in 1999 and since 2004 judges have been trained in human rights legislation as Turkey prepares to submit itself to the rulings of the European Court of Human Rights. Free speech is

A Delicate Subject

Most subjects are freely discussed amongst Turks and, as a visitor, you may be asked your opinion on topical subjects. Don't be afraid to speak up, but one word of caution: the flag, Atatürk and the army are sensitive subjects not always understood by foreigners. It is a punishable crime to insult the Turkish flag or Atatürk, even in jest. The armed forces are regarded as Turkey's secular sentinels and compulsory military service is part of the national ethos for all males over 18 years old. Kurdish independence or any issues which seem to threaten Turkish solidarity or destabilize the State are best avoided unless you know Turkey well and can speak passable Turkish.

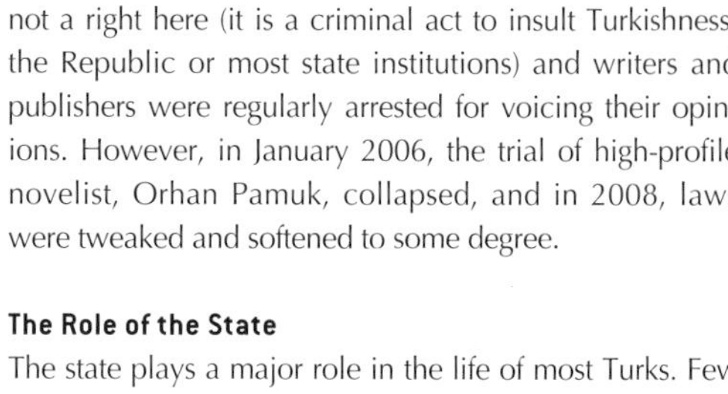

not a right here (it is a criminal act to insult Turkishness, the Republic or most state institutions) and writers and publishers were regularly arrested for voicing their opinions. However, in January 2006, the trial of high-profile novelist, Orhan Pamuk, collapsed, and in 2008, laws were tweaked and softened to some degree.

The Role of the State

The state plays a major role in the life of most Turks. Few regard it as subservient to the electorate – most citizens accept the state as an avuncular provider whom they feel honoured to serve and, often, obey. Most civil servants are accustomed to a short working life and a level of perks and job security which would be intolerable elsewhere.

Many services and key industries are still state run. The road to privatization has been a slow and often tortuous one, with little real political will to follow through. However, it has finally reached the point where there is more private than state ownership of industry, and the programme continues.

Turkey and the European Union

Since 1952, Turkey has been a loyal member of NATO. In 1959, Turkey signed the Treaty of Rome, making her an associate member of the European Community. Turkey was admitted to the European Customs Union in January 1996 and has since been pushing hard for full membership of the European Union. The fact that many other countries (including Greek Cyprus) were allowed to join while Turkey remained out in the cold as is seen by many as a direct insult. However, there have been changes in the courts and human rights in an effort to overcome some of the more obvious hurdles; the Turks have made overtures to the Greek Cypriots (all rejected so far) in an effort to sort out the Cyprus question, and substantive talks on possible membership have now begun. Nevertheless, many in Europe (including Germany) remain adamantly opposed to Turkish membership on economic grounds while others feel that this largely Asian, Muslim country simply does not fit. Meantime, many within Turkey are

Economic Figures

The Turkish Gross National Product (GNP) escalated rapidly after Atatürk's 1922 takeover. By 1924 the GNP was growing at a rate of 15%. By the end of the decade this had risen to 22%. As a result of the World Slump, growth collapsed to 11% in 1932. After World War II the economy recovered, to grow at a slow but steady rate of 4–8%. The crash of the lira in the late 1990s pushed the growth rate into double figures, but after several years at around a steady 5%, it took a sharp nosedive, slowing to 0.9% in 2008 and actually shrinking by 5.6% in 2009. By 2011, it had bounced back spectacularly to a growth rate of 8.5%.

now beginning to question whether they really still want to join, and are looking to realign themselves with the Islamic states and newly emerging powers such as India and Brazil and Africa which they believe would better serve their political and economic interests.

▲ *Above: Colourful ceramic plates on display.*
◀ *Opposite: Watermelons for sale, a familiar sight on city streets in summer.*

Industry and Commerce

Many come to Turkey to see ancient ruins. But few are prepared for Turkey's dynamic industrial growth, which has gone from strength to strength in spite of the global financial crisis, achieving 9.2% growth in 2011. Exports reached a high of US$143.4 billion the same year. Textiles, particularly ready-to-wear garments, scooped up around a third of the total. Many factories are also turning out vital components for European and US-branded manufacturers with names like IKEA, Marks and Spencer, Levi's, Sears and Walmart all sourcing directly or indirectly on the Turkish market (although this is now under pressure with the end of a global quota system that has cushioned them from direct competition until recently). The satellite suburbs of Istanbul boast state-of-the-art factories and industrial parks. Huge investments have been made in machinery and technology. Textiles, automobiles and parts, ceramic tiles, household appliances, furniture, hazelnuts and leather are top exports. The Customs Union allows goods to pass without duties to and from Turkey to all European countries, giving them a big advantage over Far Eastern rivals.

Like the rest of the world, Turkey has had its share of economic woes and homegrown problems from corruption, the ongoing Kurdish unrest and huge debts to contend with, exacerbated by international events from the Arab Spring to the global financial recession. However, the Turks have proved they are resilient. The lira has remained stable, inflation remains relatively low and unemployment isn't out of control. With relatively little debt and mortgage in comparison to the western world, the Turkish banking and finance sector rode the storm in remarkably good shape. The privatization of state industries is well underway and private sector businesses are

Up There With the Best

Turkey is learning more about the rest of the world through defence contracts than almost any other way. Turkish Aerospace Industries started from the bottom in 1984 and now fighter jets made to US Air Force specifications are sold to other nations. Partner firms include Lockheed Martin and Sikorsky. Over 300 different types of aircraft are produced along with helicopters, unmanned airborne surveillance vehicles and navigation systems.

adept at implementing state-of-the-art technology. New pipelines coming onstream are helping to channel Central Asian oil across the country, paying their passage and removing supertankers from the overcrowded Bosphorus. The country is well poised to take advantage of the upturn once the Western economies recover and begin to look for imports again. This vibrant market has found its feet and is powering forward and with huge amounts of room left for development and growth domestically, the future is looking very rosy indeed.

Turkey's Alcatraz

The capture of PKK strongman, **Abdullah Öcalan**, was recorded as one of Turkey's most glorious triumphs. Tracked to Kenya by Security Forces in March 1999, Öcalan is the sole inmate on **Imralı Island** in the **Marmara Sea**. The jail and courthouse were renovated to accommodate him. Even grazing animals had to be removed from the island, as it was declared a military zone. Öcalan's trial focused much attention on the Turkish judicial and legal system and led to the repeal of the death penalty in Turkey due to pressure from the EU.

Tourism

Tourism is one of Turkey's most important industries. Since 1999, the country has faced a series of setbacks such as the Istanbul earthquake, the Kosovo War, the PKK's terrorist campaigns, the devastation of September 11th, the war in Iraq, the Istanbul bombs and, most recently, the Syrian crisis. However, passion for this magnificent land has proved remarkable and numbers have not only recovered after each crisis, but have continued to rise. Some 30.1 million people visited the country in 2011, continuing the staggering growth in popularity Turkey has achieved in recent years. With Istanbul celebrating its status as European City of Culture throughout 2010 and Turkey cashing in both from price hikes in the euro zone and new emerging markets in the east, the success looks set to continue for some time.

The Turkoman People

Turkoman people, from whom the Turks are descended, still exist throughout the Middle East (especially in Iran, Syria and Afghanistan). The largest concentration (2.7 million) live in the Republic of Turkmenistan, on the eastern shore of the Caspian Sea, which came into being in 1991 after the collapse of the former Soviet Union.

The Kurdish Question

To much of the world, the Kurdish question is about human rights and the solution is to grant the Kurdish population the autonomy and democracy they have been agitating for for 20 years. In fact a large percentage of the 14.5 million Kurds in Turkey have already integrated into the mainstream of Turkish working and social life. It has been the radical Kurdistan Worker's Party (PKK) who have demanded their own land, language and media. Their tactics have been violent and the group resorted to extortion as well as smuggling drugs and arms to finance their cause. They have many sympathizers inside and outside Turkey, including a large number of unwilling ones.

Turkey sees a group determined to divide the state and has spent billions of dollars and manpower defending territory she almost lost after World War I – territory that also happens to be extremely rich in both water and oil. The cost of defending Turkey's territorial integrity is high with around 40,000 lives lost (most of them Kurds). Meantime, many more billions are being thrown into developing the resources of the region and resettling Turks in a patchwork of booming new towns and villages.

The future? When educational standards rise and prosperity replaces poverty, neighbours will cultivate their gardens instead of squabbling over who owns the wall.

Safety Tip

Sophistication and prosperity have brought a few less welcome elements to coastal areas. There is zero tolerance to **drugs**, using or peddling. You may find some Turks get away with it (*Türkiye böyle* means 'that's how it goes in Turkey') but, as a foreigner, you will not. Never accept food offered by strangers. Smiling hangers-on may offer you sweets or drinks containing a mild sedative. One unfortunate visitor arrived at a local police stations with nothing but his 'smalls'! The culprits are usually Iranians or Iraqis, not Turks. Intercity bus companies issue the same warning on journeys.

THE PEOPLE

The Turks include a rich **ethnic mix**. Over the past millennia, countless peoples, native invaders and settlers have left their racial mark on the nation. These mainly included the **Greeks**, **Kurds**, **Armenians**, **Persians** and **Mongols**. The **Turkoman** people began arriving in Anatolia from central Asia in the 11th century, and within 400 years had completely occupied the country integrating with the older inhabitants.

Further ethnic mixing took place during the Ottoman Empire, when several Turkic groups living in the Caucasus and around the Black Sea migrated into Anatolia.

The result of all this is that the Turkish people include a wide range of racial types. Although dark-haired Turkic–Mediterranean types predominate, it is not unusual to see several blond, blue-eyed Turks, Turks with hooded, Asiatic eyes, and Turks with a distinctly Arabic appearance. Skin colours range from fair to sallow (the predominant colouring) and dark. There are even red-haired Turks with freckles, a legacy of the invasion of the **Galatians**, who are thought to have been of Celtic origin.

◀ Opposite: Turkey's varied coastline provides a perfect playground for a booming tourism sector.
▼ Below: Traditional water pipes are a feature of Turkish café society.

HISTORICAL CROSSCURRENTS

Whilst unsuccessfully attempting to form a coalition government after the general election in April 1999, a leading politician was interviewed on the BBC. Asked why the problem of agreeing on a government should be such a difficult task, he explained it like this: 'You see, in Turkey, we are not just dealing with one homogeneous group of people. Some Turks are still living in the 19th century, others are living in the 20th century, and then there are the Turks who cannot wait to be in the 21st century.' This summarizes a lot about Turkey, well beyond the political sphere.

Despite all this racial intermingling, there remain two distinct minority groups: the Kurds, and to a lesser extent the Arabs. The Kurds account for around 20% of the population, with their main concentration in the remote eastern section of the country. True **Arabs** are found almost exclusively in the southeast of the country, and make up less than 1% of the population. The main cities still have small communities of Turkish Jews, Greeks and Armenians.

Daily Life

In practice, Turkey is a class-layered society like any other. The two most decisive factors are much the same as those elsewhere – money and education. However, you will notice a marked distinction between urban and rural dwellers. Life in villages and small towns has altered little for decades. **Segregation** of the sexes is rigorously adhered to and local and religious customs are passed on intact through successive generations. Marriages are arranged, although dowries these days often include washing machines and other household appliances. Men go to coffee houses and women crochet and gossip when their work is done. The family is a close-knit unit but, increasingly, newlyweds opt for their own house, not their parents', if they can afford it. Even in villages, if a young girl finds work her family considers suitable, she will often delay or forsake marriage in place of freedom and independence. A traditional village wedding begins on a Friday and ends on the Sunday when the bride is officially brought from her family home to her new husband's. A village wedding is an expansive and joyous affair and, if you are asked to join in, don't miss it.

Life in the big cities is not much different from that in Europe. BMWs and Jeeps flash by, fast food is consumed at McDonald's and nightlife is glamorous. A new hypermarket culture has emerged in Istanbul's outlying districts and a visit to Planet, Continent or Metro will give you a much better insight into Turkish life than strolling around Taksim Square. Over 60% of Turkey's youth are under 30 years old, which accounts for their dynamic shopping patterns. Shopping malls like Akmerkez and Carousel are teeming with all tastes and brand names.

As in Europe, mobile phones have become a 'must have' – and almost everyone does. They are called *cep* (pocket) phones and the main operator, Turkcell, has reciprocal roaming contracts with over 100 countries worldwide.

▲ Above: A schoolchild lays a wreath of flowers at Atatürk's tomb.

◀ Opposite: Provincial life: women washing carpets in the river below the citadel at Kars.

Education and Employment

Only about 10% of the Turkish population were literate at the formation of the Republic in 1923. Today, 87.4% of the country is literate, a remarkable achievement set in motion by Atatürk. In 1997, the government enacted the compulsory eight-year education law, effectively raising the school-leaving age to 15 years. However, teachers, particularly in rural areas, were in short supply and the student to teacher ratio is very high. The move angered religious elements that found their Islamic religious academies empty and secular studies supplanting religious ones.

The state keeps a tight rein on the educational curriculum at all levels. There are many state and provincial universities, and dozens of privately run colleges, high schools and universities have sprung up in the more affluent western provinces. However, universities are overcrowded and the competition for a university place has become positively brutal. The raising of fees at state universities has caused disruption and social unrest. For all this, education has a low priority today on government budgets, and families who can, sacrifice much to educate their offspring at universities in the USA or Great Britain.

High unemployment rates have not helped to guarantee jobs – or good pay – for graduates. Raising the retirement age to European levels was the cause of much strife, as Turks' life expectancy is lower than that in Europe or the USA.

The Turkish Language

A number of Turkish words are phonetic renderings of their European equivalent. Here are a few examples you are likely to come across:

Büfe • Buffet

Beysbol • A popular American game

Şarküteri • Charcuterie (prepared meat)

Kuaför • Coiffure (ladies' hairdresser)

Psikiyatrist • For those with mental problems

Feribot • Ferry

Milyon • 1,000,000

▲ *Above: Though laid on specially for visitors, performances at Ephesus give a flavour of traditional Turkish folk dance.*

Religion

During the Ottoman era, **Muslim** religion and state affairs were closely identified. In 1923 Atatürk decreed a new **secular state**. However, despite this separation of religion and state, 99% of modern Turks are Muslims. The majority of Turkish Muslims are orthodox **Sunnis**, with the remainder being **Shi'ite**. Most Turks take a fairly moderate attitude toward their religion. Alcohol, shunned by the more devout Muslims, is widely available and the majority of Turks no longer publicly observe the five daily calls to prayer. Despite this generally relaxed attitude, most Turks remain devout and are sensitive to comments about Islam. There is also a new awareness of religion becoming obvious throughout the country, thanks to the highly organized popularity of the AKP, who are helping both the poor and middle-class businessmen. Increasing numbers of women are choosing to wear headscarves, partly as a fashion statement, leaving only the intellectuals to question where it is all leading.

Festivals

The main festivals of the Turkish year follow the Muslim calendar. **Ramazan** (or Ramadan) is marked by 40 days of fasting, food only being eaten during the hours between sunset and sunrise. Ramazan is followed by **Şeker Bayramı** (the Sugar Festival), when families and relatives exchange sweets. **Kurban Bayramı**, the Feast of Sacrifice, echoing Abraham's sacrifice of his son, follows 68 days after the end of Ramazan. Families buy a live sheep or lamb, which is then slaughtered (often in the street) accompanied by prayers and singing, after which the meat is usually distributed to the poor. A word of warning: try to avoid travelling during these times as all modes of transport are fully booked and the roads clogged. Traffic accidents are the scourge of the country.

Classical Music

Turkish classical music dates from the Ottoman era, and has developed a distinctive and subtle style of its own. The best place to listen is at one of the Sunday morning concerts given in Istanbul by *Klâsik Icra Heyeti*. The traditional instruments – the *ud*, the *saz* and the *kanun* – sound primitive, eastern and agonizingly sad. Like English humour, the semitones and rhythms can grow on you.

Cultural Life

Turkey's rich cultural tradition has absorbed influences from many sources. The first Turkoman people were little more than **nomadic** tribesmen, with a primitive way of life and a loose animist religion. By the 11th century they had taken on the Muslim religion, and absorbed the first elements of Persian and Arabic culture. The remnant Byzantine civilization added a new inspiration, particularly in architecture. But the Ottoman Turks quickly transcended this, developing a superb architecture of their own, which reached its peak in the construction of the great mosques. When the Ottoman Empire expanded into eastern Europe, it absorbed certain European traits. Then, with the collapse of the sultanate in the early years of the 20th century, modern European influences prevailed. The transformation of Turkish by means of a European alphabet played a major part in encouraging writers to look to Europe for modernistic inspiration, rather than to the more arcane culture of the Middle East.

Yılmaz Güney

One of Turkey's foremost film-makers was Yılmaz Güney who died in 1984. Güney was a leftist and, though his films seem innocuous today, in the 1960s and 1970s they were deemed contentious and banned throughout Turkey. With maturity, the demise of communism and the support of Güney's widow, Turkish audiences can now enjoy his films. His masterpiece *Yol* (The Road) opened to enthusiastic audiences at Istanbul cinemas in 1998, and *Duvar* (The Wall) has been aired on several TV channels.

Craftwork

Turkish carpets and **kilims** are renowned throughout the world. Prices vary according to the material the carpet is woven from, how closely it is woven, the quality of the dyes, the expertise of the craftsman, and the complexity of the design. A word of warning: smuggling any antique or carpet over 100 years old out of Turkey is a serious crime. Few kilims are this old but a reputable seller will provide you with a certificate from a museum stating that your purchase is not an antique.

Traditionally the finest Turkish **ceramics** came from Iznik. Many modern reproductions are exquisite and marvellously decorated with fine colours and glazes. **Copperware**, **leather goods**, **alabaster** and **Meerschaum pipes** are worth looking for. As with all tourist-oriented goods, quality ranges from superb to plain awful. Fortunately, the better quality goods predominate, and there are usually bargains to be had, if you're willing to do a bit of friendly haggling.

▼ *Below: Designs in flat-weave kilims often include stylized birds and animals.*

Football Mania

The Turks are obsessed with sport – especially football. At weekends, and during mid-week matches, life grinds to a virtual halt. What appears to be the entire male population of the nation watches TV – at home, in cafés, through shop windows – anywhere. It's never difficult to tell when the home team is winning, as being a spectator is not a passive activity in Turkey. The country's three giant international teams, Galatasaray, Beşiktaş, and Fenerbahçe, are all based in Istanbul.

Sport and Recreation

Football is Turkey's most popular sport, encouraged by media hype, sponsorship and transfer fees – much like anywhere else. However, Turkey's official national sport is **oil wrestling** (*see* page 51). **Camel wrestling** takes place in Muğla, Izmir and Antalya provinces in February and March. In eastern Turkey, **cirit**, a symbolic and traditional jousting match played on horseback, is thrilling and colourful.

Basketball has almost as much star appeal as football, and volleyball is extremely competitive for both men's and women's leagues. In big cities, people fit sports like swimming, horseback riding and tennis into their daily life for enjoyment or to keep fit.

Recreation of a different sort is a **Turkish bath**, or *hamam*. The traditional ones like Çemberlitaş, in Sultanahmet, are just that – traditional. They are fun but for real luxury and no hanky panky, there is nothing to compare to the luxury hotels whose *hamams* are generally open to non-residents.

At coastal resorts, **water sports** abound. The main diving centres at Bodrum and Kaş are heavily booked during the high season. But other sports are gradually being promoted, and sports like whitewater rafting, skiing, trekking, mountaineering and hot-air ballooning (mostly in Cappadocia) are well organized and regulated.

▶ *Opposite: Traditional fare: coffee, sticky baklava and Turkish Delight.*
▼ *Below: The domed interior of a Turkish bath.*

Food and Drink

The Turkish nomads of central Asia may have had little time for the delicate niceties of the kitchen, but they still bequeathed to the world three important culinary inventions. *Şiş* consists of small pieces of skewered meat which are cooked over an open fire. These **kebabs** made an ideal meal for a people on the move. Those on an even faster trot and with even less time didn't cook their meat

at all. The Tartar people gave us 'steak tartare'. **Yoghurt**, nowadays an essential ingredient and used in a wide variety of dishes, was also introduced by Turkic tribes.

Sophistication was added to the Turkish kitchen after the fall of Constantinople in the mid-15th century, when the Ottomans added the exotic delicacies of their Byzantine cuisine. Stuffed vegetables – such as aubergines and peppers – were soon a favourite, as were various spicy rice dishes, vine leaves, and many sickly sweet cakes.

The most obvious manifestation of the regional delights offered by the Turkish kitchen is *mezes*. These *hors d'oeuvres* include dishes like *humus* (a tasty chickpea dish), stuffed vine leaves, fiery garlic yoghurt and goat's cheese pastie – and they taste as exciting as they look.

Kebab salons tempt with a mouthwatering variety of kebabs, usually called *kebap* in Turkey.

Sticky, sweet cakes such as baklava or *burma kadayıf* come soaked in honey are usually eaten at pastry shops rather than at the end of a meal.

The best way to round off your meal is with a small, strong Turkish **coffee**. Avoid drinking right to the bottom of the cup, which is invariably grainy. **Alcohol** is readily available throughout Turkey, although less so in eastern regions and in religious cities like Bursa or Konya. Turks are champion beer drinkers and, as well as the local *Efes Pilsen* brand on draft or in bottles, international brews can be found. Turkey makes a few outstanding wines amongst a myriad of passable or just plain characterless ones. The local drink, usually to accompany meals, is **rakı**, or lion's milk. It has an aniseed flavour and turns cloudy with the addition of water but has a kick like a mule.

Turkish Water

The Ottomans had a passion for fresh, sweet water and savoured it like wine. Some experts knew from which spring the water had come. Unfortunately, the same is not true today. In an effort to minimize municipal expenditure, chlorine levels are often reduced and while most water in big cities is probably safe, everybody drinks bottled water, which is cheap and universally available.

Turkish Coffee and Tea

Turkish coffee is served in tiny cups. It is usually quite strong and the bottom of the cup will have a muddy residue which is best left. Nowadays Turkey imports most of its coffee from Brazil, and, owing to inflation and devaluation of the Turkish lira, the price has shot up. In cafés the most popular drink at present is tea, which comes in a small bulb-shaped glass.

2
Istanbul

Technically, Istanbul lies divided, its European side separated from its Asian outskirts by the **Bosphorus** channel – vital waterlink between the Black Sea and the oceans of the world. Yet, as soon as you set foot in the city, there's no mistaking that you're in the East. It's not just the profusion of magnificent mosques, or the exotic bustle of the bazaars. The music is different, so are the people, and though the writing on the shopfronts may be in the European alphabet, it certainly looks strange.

The Old City of Istanbul (*Stamboul*), from where the sultans once ruled an empire that stretched from the Gates of Vienna to the Indian Ocean, stands on a hillside overlooking water on three sides. To the north lies the inlet known as the **Golden Horn**, to the south the blue waters of the enclosed Sea of Marmara, and to the east the mighty Bosphorus, which is now spanned by two modern suspension bridges, the Boğazici (Bosphorus) Bridge and the Fatih Sultan Mehmet Bridge. There are few sights to match a crescent moon rising above the domes and minarets of Istanbul, its reflection melting into the dark waters below. The best place to watch the spectacular Istanbul sunsets is from chic Bebek, or else from a café in upbeat Ortaköy.

If you feel the need to take a break from the commotion of Istanbul, you can take a ferry to the **Princes' Islands** (*see* page 45) or go for a picnic in the **Belgrade Forest**. Best of all, go out to **Polonezköy**. All these are within the Istanbul municipal area but far enough away to be refreshing.

Don't Miss

****** Topkapı Palace:** from here the sultans ruled their empire. Home of the dazzling Spoonmaker's diamond.
****** Aya Sofya:** for almost 1000 years the most famous church in Christendom, called the Eye of the Universe.
****** The Blue Mosque:** one of the great mosques of Istanbul.
****** The Dolmabahçe Palace:** the 19th-century sultans' homage to excess.
*** The City Walls:** walls which once guarded the ancient Byzantium.

◀ *Opposite: The domes and minarets of Istanbul capture the mystery of the East.*

Visiting Topkapi

The Topkapı is open 09:00–17:00 (to 19:00 in summer), closed Tue; www.topkapisarayi.gov.tr There are separate tickets and an additional fee for the Harem, which can only be visited on a guided tour. Queues build up fast, so get a timed ticket from the ticket office near the Harem entrance and visit the rest of the palace while waiting.

SIGHTSEEING IN THE OLD CITY

The streets of Istanbul reflect a rather haphazard blend of ancient and modern. Car horns compete with transistor radios and mobile telephones. Old men, ceaselessly fingering long strings of worry beads, share a *hookah* pipe at the café, while their sons sit glued to the TV screens watching football. Strictly dressed fundamentalist young women mingle with their 'jeans generation' peers.

In high summer the combined heat and clamour of the streets can become oppressive. An element of culture shock is inevitable: but it needn't prove to be overwhelming. Take it easy to begin with. Visit the sites early in the morning, or late in the afternoon, and stop off at the cafés for a refreshing bulb glass of tea.

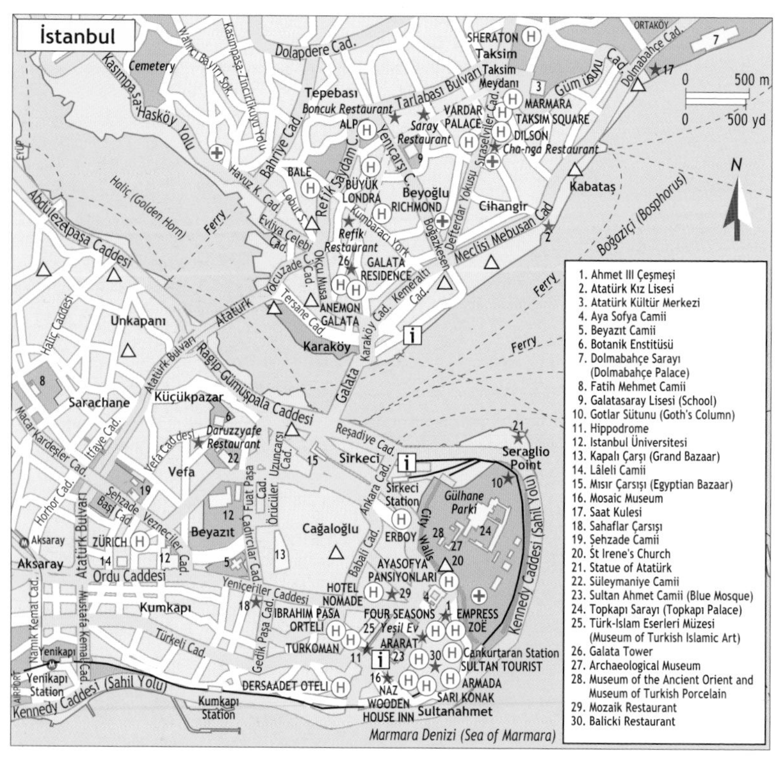

Istanbul offers a host of sights, great and small, mostly in the Old City. The following attractions are listed so that you can visit them in an easy succession from east to west across the Old City.

Topkapı Palace ★★★

The grounds of the Topkapı Palace occupy the elevated eastern end of the Old City, the **Seraglio Point**. It's a superb site, dominating the entrance to the Golden Horn, with wonderful views across the Bosphorus towards the Asian shore.

This is the palace from which the Ottoman Empire was ruled for over 400 years, frequently by its eunuchs, harem ladies and the fearsome Janissary Corps. Surprisingly, it is not an overwhelmingly grand palace, such as Versailles or Buckingham. In fact it's an unexpectedly homely place, with shady interleading courtyards, and all its components in suitable proportion. It's easy to imagine how pleasant it could have been to live here.

The Topkapı Palace was built in the mid-15th century, just a few years after the Turks had conquered the city and made it the capital of their new empire. Over the centuries many elaborate additions were commissioned, resulting in the pleasantly unsymmetrical complex of buildings and courtyards which remains today.

You enter the main section of the palace through **Ortakapı** (the Middle Gate), which leads into the large **Second Court**. The buildings located in the top left-hand corner of this courtyard are the celebrated **harem**, where visitors are required to book for guided tours. The building is now devoid of its former inhabitants, but the walls still exude the intrigue and oppression which was part of this unusual *modus vivendi*.

The One Who Got Away

Sultan Ibrahim the Mad believed in living up to his name. When he suspected one of his wives of being unfaithful to him, he flew into such a jealous rage that he ordered his entire harem to be sewn into sacks and drowned in the Bosphorus. After having been thrown overboard, only one of his wives managed to claw her way free, was rescued by a passing French ship, and managed to make her escape to France.

▼ *Below: Baghdad Köşkü in the Topkapı Palace, long-time home to the sultans.*

The Desecration of Aya Sofya

Aya Sofya has been sacked several times during its long history, but the worst indignity was inflicted in 1204, when **Crusaders** captured Byzantium and ravaged the city. The victorious Crusaders celebrated by getting drunk and installing a prostitute on the emperor's throne in the Aya Sofya.

Contrary to popular belief, the Harem was not just where the sultan kept his wives and concubines, it was also the headquarters from which he ruled his entire empire. This meant that there had to be sufficient accommodation for the various ministers, visiting generals, advisers and the like. Understandably, these quarters were strictly segregated from the Harem proper, and anyone who took the wrong turning in the maze of halls and wings would not only encounter a fierce eunuch, but was liable to become one himself.

There are many other sights at Topkapı which should not be missed. These include the fabulous decor of the **Throne Room**, in the **Third Court**. This courtyard also contains Ahmet III's superb **Library**, as well as the **Treasury**, which occupies the upper righthand corner and contains many priceless relics, including the huge **Topkapı Diamond** (sometimes known as the 'Spoonmaker's diamond').

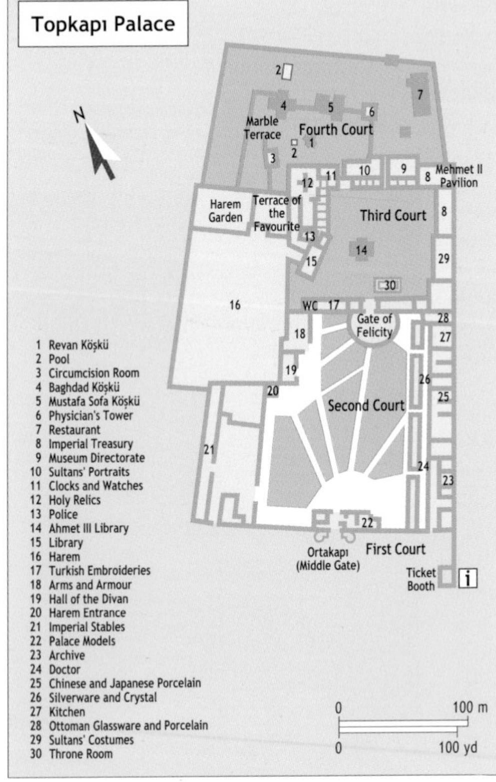

The Treasury also houses the enchanting **Mehmet II Pavilion**, whose cool, pillared terrace has one of the most romantic views of the **Bosphorus**. Beyond this is the Fourth and last Court, which looks out over the Golden Horn. This court contains the pool where Ibrahim the Mad would cavort with his harem, as well as the charming little pavilion known as the **Baghdad Köşkü** (the latter word is the origin of our word 'kiosk').

Aya Sofya ★★★

▲ *Above: Four minarets surround the central dome of Istanbul's Aya Sofya.*

The name of this massive domed red church means 'divine wisdom' in Greek. It stands on **Sultanahmet Square**, just across from the Blue Mosque, in the heart of the Old City.

Aya Sofya was built around AD535 by the Roman **Emperor Justinian**. By this time the Empire had converted to Christianity and its capital had moved here, to the glorious purpose-built city of Constantinople. The construction of Aya Sofya was so vast and ambitious a project that it is said to have taken 10,000 men almost six years to achieve, and all but bankrupted the Roman Empire. Building material used in its construction was looted from as far afield as Ephesus (in Aegean Turkey) and Baalbek (in modern-day Lebanon).

Inside its gloomy darkness, one is immediately overwhelmed by the huge, chilly inner spaces, topped by a truly awesome **dome** and often slashed by dramatic rays of sunlight. For over a thousand years this was the largest enclosed space in the world. The enormous central dome spans over 30m (100ft) and receives no support except from the massive buttresses at its rim, an amazing architectural feat at the time. In the northern aisle you can see the famous '**Weeping Column**'. Poke your finger into the well-worn hole of this pillar and make a wish.

Although Aya Sofya was sacked several times during its long history, its marvellous treasures looted or destroyed, many of the fine **mosaics** of saints and emperors have survived to this day. The finest are in the gallery above.

After the fall of the city to the Turks in 1453, Aya Sofya became a mosque, until Atatürk had it classified as a museum in 1936. Open Tue–Sun Apr–Oct 09:00–19:00, Nov–Mar 09:00–16:30.

Istanbul's History

c1200BC Mycenaen settlement established.
c600BC City is founded by Greek colonists under their leader Byzas, after whom the city is named Byzantium.
c500BC Byzantium besieged by invading Persian army.
c300BC City taken by Philip of Macedon (father of Alexander the Great).
c100 Byzantium sacked by Emperor Septimus Severus.
c300 Emperor Constantine moves capital of Roman Empire to Byzantium and renames it Constantinople.
1204 Constantinople sacked by Crusaders.
1453 Constantinople overrun by Ottoman Turks and renamed Islamboul.
1920 Atatürk relocates Turkey's capital to Ankara.
1930 City's name officially changed to Istanbul.

▲ *Above: The magnificent domed interior ceiling of the Blue Mosque.*
▶ *Opposite: The Grand Bazaar consists of several different atmospheric markets or districts.*

The Blue Mosque ★★★

Known by the Turks as the **Sultan Ahmet Camii**, this is the magnificent mosque across the square from Aya Sofya, which dominates the Old City skyline, overlooking the Sea of Marmara, the Golden Horn and the Bosphorus. It was built in the early 17th century.

As you approach from the northeast you see the complex multidomed structure rising to the central dome, overlooked by six slender **minarets**, each with three circular balconies. These few slim towers caused great consternation when they were built, for it meant that the Blue Mosque now had as many minarets as the chief mosque at Mecca. Rather than destroy the pleasing symmetry of the Blue Mosque, the sultan overcame this problem by having a seventh minaret built at Islam's holiest mosque at Mecca.

Inside, the walls are covered with over 20,000 blue Iznik tiles, and the arches are inscribed with decorative Arabic calligraphy. The domes are supported by massive 'Elephant's Foot' pillars, and the high enclosed space illuminated by stained-glass windows. It is important to remember that, when entering any mosque in Turkey, you must always remove your shoes. Women should cover their heads and their arms, and not wear revealing dresses or shorts. The Blue Mosque is open daily from 09:00–19:00, except during prayer times (visit early in the morning).

The Hippodrome ★★

This ancient Roman arena, which once seated up to 100,000 spectators, stands in the shadow of the Blue Mosque. The track which ran around its edges was over 1000m (1100yd) long, and was used for chariot races, which were immensely popular in ancient Byzantium. Important events attracted attendances as large as those at major modern football matches.

Iznik Tiles

Nowadays, Iznik (see page 57) is just a small lakeside town southeast of Istanbul. During the 15th century, Mehmet I brought some 500 captured potters from Persia to Iznik, who introduced the secrets of their art into Turkey. The result was a flourishing trade in exquisitely hand-decorated tiles, many of which contained a copper blue which had hitherto been unobtainable outside Persia. At its height, over 300 kilns produced ceramics and tiles here, which were transported throughout the Ottoman Empire to decorate mosques and other buildings.

The Hippodrome was originally laid out in the 3rd century. Today, little remains of its former glory, except the columns in the centre of the track. No one knows the origins of the **Column of Constantine VII Porphryogenitus**, whose bronze plates were taken to Venice by Crusaders in 1204. The **Serpent Column** was made in the 5th century BC from the melted-down shields of the defeated Persian army and stood in Delphi. The **Egyptian Obelisk** was created in the 15th century BC during the reign of Pharaoh Thutmose III. It was pillaged in the 4th century AD during the reign of Emperor Theodosius I and was broken in transit, but the hieroglyphs remain clearly visible.

Ancient Hooliganism

The crowds at the Hippodrome chariot races were notorious for their partisanship. Each race featured two contestants, one wearing a blue, the other a green emblem. The crowd's loyalty was divided between the BLUES and the GREENS, giving fanatical support to their chosen colour. Frequent riots erupted between the opposing factions, which sometimes brought the entire city to a standstill. On one occasion, fighting was so prolonged and violent that much of the city was razed to the ground and the main church was reduced to a mass of charred rubble. This was the site chosen for Aya Sofya.

The Sunken Palace ★★

The magical **Basilica Cistern** (Yerebatan Sarayı) in Sultanahmet Square was the water source for the Topkapı Palace and the Grand Palace of the Byzantines. A vast palacial cavern of Byzantine arches held up by ancient columns, it is open 09:00–17:30 daily (longer in summer); www.yerebatan.com

The Grand Bazaar ★★★

Known in Turkish as the **Kapalı Çarşı**, it is the largest covered bazaar in the world. After Mehmet the Conqueror took Constantinople from the Christian Byzantines in 1453, he set about transforming the city into the capital of his new Islamic empire. To entice traders back into the deserted city and stimulate its stagnant economy, priority was given to the building of this bazaar, and it was completed well before the Topkapı Palace and the city's first new mosque.

Over the centuries the Grand Bazaar suffered many catastrophes. It burnt down several times, and was reduced to a huge field of rubble after an earthquake. The bazaar may at first appear to be a maze-like jumble of alleyways, but is in fact laid out on a clear grid pattern. This layout divides the bazaar into separate districts, which specialize in different goods.

The Sultan's Wrath

In the 15th century, when the **plague** reached Istanbul, the **Grand Bazaar** was rapidly closed to prevent the spread of this dreaded disease. Sultan Mehmet II's guard enforced this decree by surrounding the bazaar, scimitars drawn. It was several months before the bazaar was reopened, only to reveal that the entire quarters had been looted of all their merchandise. As punishment for the inefficient protection, the sultan ordered that his guard be decimated, and one in every 10 was beheaded.

More Istanbul

With a city this ancient and rich in history and culture, and a book this small, we cannot hope to provide a definitive guide in one chapter, although we've done our best to cram in the many highlights. For more detailed information, consult the ***Globetrotter Guide to Istanbul*** or websites such as http://english.istanbul.com or www.theguideistanbul.com

The central **Iç Bedesten** (the Old Market) specializes in antiques, silverware and copper items. South of here, along **Keseciler Caddesi**, are the bag shops. To the west of Iç Bedesten is **Takkecilar Sokak**, where you can find yet more antiques and silverware. The oldest part of the Bazaar is **Sahaflar Çarşısı**, a corner of which has been devoted to selling ancient books since Byzantine times. Other streets used to be named after the trade which was practised in them: Sword-makers' Street, Jewellers' Alley and so forth. Nowadays many of these trades have moved elsewhere.

The Bazaar can get hot and crowded, and pickpockets know every trick. But you're never far from a cold-drink stand or fountain. Many of the stallholders are genuinely friendly and enjoy **bargaining** with you over a cup of Turkish tea. And for your part, there are all kinds of bargains to be had – from excellent leather accessories to carpets and gold and silver jewellery. Open 09:00–19:00, Monday–Saturday.

Süleymaniye Mosque ★★

This mosque is in the northwestern sector of the Old City, looking down over the Fatih Sultan Mehmet (formerly Galata) Bridge across the **Golden Horn**.

Many architectural historians consider this to be the finest mosque to be built by **Mimar Sinan**, the greatest Turkish architect. He designed it in the mid-16th century, at the peak of the Ottoman Empire, for **Süleyman the Magnificent**. Over 5000 excellent workmen were employed in its construction. The superb stained-glass windows were made by Ibrahim the Drunkard. The external proportions of the mosque are equally exquisite. Its dome and minaret stand out above the western skyline of Istanbul at sunset, when seen from the famous viewing point on the quay beside the northeastern end of Fatih Sultan Mehmet Bridge. The interior was restored in the 19th century by two Swiss architects, the Fossati brothers. They saw fit to accentuate its purity of line with various Baroque flourishes, a

desecration which has reduced many architectural critics to stunned silence.

The mosque's graveyard contains Süleyman's tomb. Beside him is buried his much-feared wife **Roxelana**, who exercised an ever-increasing influence over him – finally persuading him to murder the heir to the throne, so that her own son could succeed instead. Open daily except at prayer times.

At the corner of the nearby street which is named after Mimar Sinan, you can see the great architect's burial place in a tomb which he designed for himself.

▲ Above: This section of the Old City wall guarded the European approaches to the city.
◀ Opposite: Süleymaniye Mosque, floodlit at night.

The Old City Walls ★

The site was originally chosen by the Greeks around 3000 years ago, because of its superbly defensible position. The earliest city stood on the high promontory now occupied by the grounds of Topkapı Palace. The only defence then installed was a short land wall crossing from the Golden Horn to the Marmara shore. As the city grew, expanding up the peninsula, the fortifications gradually moved further west. Roman defensive walls ran by the Hippodrome.

The massive walls which still dominate the western approaches to the Old City were erected by the Emperor **Theodosius II** in the 5th century. Even today, with gaps at the gates widened to allow modern roads to pass through, these walls make a forbidding sight. It was over 500 years before the walls gave way to an enemy. In the 13th century Crusaders sailed up the Golden Horn, ran their ships alongside, and scaled the walls with ladders. Two hundred years later, they were more decisively breached by Mehmet II.

You can drive along the full 6km (4-mile) length of these walls. Only two towers remain standing of **Ayvan Saray**, the castle which guarded the northern end of the wall. The last Byzantine emperor, Constantine XI, rode out from this castle in 1453 to surrender Constantinople to Sultan Mehmet II, who completed the fortress at the other end of the wall a few years after the fall of Constantinople. It is called **Yedikule**

Tulips From Istanbul

One of the most colourful events of the Istanbul year is the Tulip Festival, which takes place annually from late April until early May in the northern garden suburb of Emirgan on the western shore of the Bosphorus, halfway between the two bridges. **Sultan Ahmed III** used to hold **tulip festivals** in the Topkapı palace on moonlit nights, among a profusion of tulip-filled vases and caged canaries. Tulips originated in **Mongolia**, and came to Europe via the Ottoman Empire. Here they acquired the name *tulabend*, which means 'turban'. Our name for the flower is a corruption of this word.

▲ *Above: The Bosphorus Bridge is visible from Ortaköy, a trendy waterfront village on the European side.*

(Castle of the Seven Towers), venue of the sultans' torture chamber, part of which was known as 'The Well of Blood'.

Museums ★★★

Among the finest museums in Istanbul are undoubtedly those in the **Topkapı Palace**. Also not to be missed is the **Museum of Turkish Islamic Art**, housed in the 16th-century palace of Ibrahim Paşa on the northwest side of the Hippodrome, which contains a superb collection of ancient Turkish carpets and many exhibits illustrating how ordinary people lived in Turkey from the nomadic Mongol era to the present. Near the Blue Mosque is the **Museum of Kilims and Carpets**, where you can admire this supreme Turkish art at its finest. Further along is the **Mosaic Museum**, which contains the only surviving remnants of Justinian's imperial palace, a giant 6th-century mosaic.

A Dangerous Season

For centuries after Theodosius had ordered the construction of the massive city defences, the walls of Byzantium (now Istanbul) were considered impregnable. Ironically, the first breach in these walls was not caused by an invading army. During the freak winter of 753 it became so cold that the Bosphorus froze over. When the ice melted in spring, huge ice floes came crashing and careering down the Bosphorus on the released tide, some as tall as the city walls themselves. They smashed into the man-made defences, tearing open gaping holes in the process.

The Archaeological Museum ★★★

Just outside Topkapı's exit, this museum houses over 60,000 Graeco-Roman and Middle Eastern antiquities and artefacts – it is a gem not to be missed. The same ticket gets you into the neighbouring **Museum of Turkish Porcelain** and **Museum of the Ancient Orient**, a superb collection including, among other treasures, the city gates of Babylon. Open Tue–Sun Apr–Oct 09:00–19:00, Nov–Mar 09:00–16:30 (www.istanbularkeoloji.gov.tr/main_page). Nearby, the **Panorama 1453 History Museum** (Topkapı Şehir Parkı; open daily 08:30–17:30) offers a 360° AV experience of the Ottoman conquest of Istanbul, while the **Museum of Islamic Sciences and Technology History** (Gülhane Park; open 09:00–16:30, closed Tue) provides a fascinating insight into the historic role of Islamic scientists.

THE GOLDEN HORN

From Eminönü, below Topkapı, the Galata Bridge crosses the Golden Horn, linking old (Roman and Byzantine) and new

(14th century onwards) Istanbul. This fabled fjord was once a princely park and now cleaned up is regaining its playground status, with museums, parks, restaurants and walks.

Climate

The temperature in Istanbul seldom rises much above 30°C (86°F), even at the height of the summer. However, the crowded and noisy streets make it seem much hotter than this. **Autumn** is milder, but it often rains. In the winter it's cold, and frequently wet. **Spring** is by far the best time to visit Istanbul.

Kariye (Chora) Museum ★★★

Some of the world's finest Byzantine mosaics are to be found just outside the Edirne Gate of the old city in the Kariye Camii, formerly known as the Monastery of St Saviour in Chora. Built in the 12th century by Maria Dukaina, the mother-in-law of Emperor Alexi I Comnene, on the site of a 5th-century chapel, most of the magnificent mosaics and frescoes date to the early 14th century. Open Thu–Tue 09:30–19:00 summer, to 17:00 winter (last admission 30 minutes earlier; www.choramuseum.com).

Eyüp Sultan ★★

After Mecca and Medina, Eyüp Mosque, on the western reaches of the Golden Horn, is considered one of the holiest in Islam. It was built in the 15th century to commemorate the death of one of the Prophet Mohammed's standard bearers, and houses his tomb. It is a sacred place for Muslims and respectful dress is obligatory. A cable car swings over the cemetery up the steep hill to **Pierre Loti's Café**, which was the house where he conducted his clandestine relationship with a Turkish woman, Aziyadé. From this romantic vantage point, his motives seem justified. No alcohol is served at the *koşk* (pavillion), as it is near the Mosque.

The **Rahmi M Koç Museum** (Hasköy Caddesi) is a fine private museum of science, technology and transport, housed in an old iron foundry. Open Tue–Fri 10:00–17:00, Sat–Sun 10:00–20:00 (Apr–Oct), Sat–Sun 10:00–18:00 (Nov–Mar), www.rmkmuseum.org.tr/english/index.html

Also on the shores of the Golden Horn is a children's park, **Miniatürk** (Imrahor Caddesi, Sütluce; open daily 09:00–17:00, admission charge, www.miniaturk.com.tr/en/category.php?id=1), with miniature models of all Turkey's most famous buildings.

More Museums

Near the mouth of the Golden Horn, in a converted warehouse, **Istanbul Modern** (Meclis-I Mebusan Caddesi Liman Sahası, Karaköy) has a permanent collection of modern Turkish art, regular exhibitions, an art house cinema and trendy café bar with superb views. Open Tue–Sun 10:00–18:00, Thu 10:00–20:00, www.istanbulmodern.org/en
The **Naval Museum** (Iskele Caddesi, Beşiktaş) has royal barges, charts and memorabilia dating back to when the Ottoman Empire was one of the world's greatest maritime powers. Open Wed–Sun 09:00–17:00, www.denizmuzeleri.tsk.tr/en/idmk/
A little way inland, the **Military Museum** (Vali Konaği Caddesi, Harbiye) follows the Turkish army from the Ottoman conquest of Constantinople to the present day. Open Wed–Sun 09:00–17:00; a Janissary band plays each afternoon at 15:00 and 16:00 in summer. Further up the shore, near Buyukdere, the **Sadberk Hanım Museum** is a private collection of archaeology, ethnography and Turkish decorative arts in two 19th-century wooden villas. Open 10:00–17:00, closed Wed, www.sadberkhanimmuzesi.org.tr/default.asp?hl=en **Sakip Sabancı Museum** (Istinye Caddesi, Emirgan) is a private museum with rooms kept as they were when the family lived here and a fine collection of decorative arts, Ottoman calligraphy, and paintings by leading Turkish artists. Open Tue–Sun 10:00–18:00; Wed 10:00–20:00, http://muze.sabanciuniv.edu/homepage

THE BOSPHORUS

Even if your stay is short, try to fit in a Bosphorus cruise. Failing that, take the number 40 bus from Taksim Square to Sarıyer and most of the way up the European (*Rumeli*) side of the Bosphorus. Turks know this river as the *Boğaziçi* and it is a crucial strategic link for Russia to gain access to the Aegean Sea from the Black Sea. Free passage is granted to all ships by the Montreux Convention of 1936 but nobody could have predicted the enormity of the giant crude oil tankers that would pass, or the volume of shipping traffic plying the dangerous, narrow passage. A shipping accident in the Bosphorus (and there have been some near misses) would be a catastrophe for Istanbul.

Dolmabahçe Palace ★★★

This modern palace stands outside the Old City, on the west bank of the Bosphorus. Built in 1853, it was used as official residence by the last sultans. It is set on a historic site – that of

◀ *Left: You can buy an elegant traditional Turkish tea set at the Grand Bazaar.*
◀◀ *Opposite: The Grand Stairway of the Dolmabahçe Palace, the last residence of the sultans.*

the harbour from which Mehmet II launched his successful attack on Constantinople in 1453. In the early 17th century **Sultan Ahmet I** had the cove filled in (an operation requiring 16,000 Christian slaves) and the site was turned into a royal garden. The Turkish word *Dolmabahçe* means 'filled-in garden'. Two hundred years later, **Sultan Abdul Mejid** chose this as the site for his new palace. Compared with Topkapı, it is grandiose, Victorian and rather dark. Queen Victoria herself contributed one of its most ostentatious features – a colossal cut-glass chandelier weighing over 4½ tons (4500kg), which hangs from the ceiling of the **Throne Room**. Beneath this glitterball the sultans were consulted on affairs of state.

The 80-minute tour includes Sultan Abdul Aziz's bed – a huge one large enough to support his massive frame as well as several members of his harem. In 1923, the palace became Atatürk's residence, and contains the room in which he died on 10 November 1938. Open 09:00–16:00 (15:00 Oct–Feb) daily, except Mon and Thu (guided tours only).

SHOPPING AND NIGHTLIFE

The best place to go shopping is the Grand Bazaar, with its large range of carpets and kilims, jewellery, silver and copperware, leather goods and antiques. The **bookmarket** in nearby Sahaflar Carşişi is noted for its antique copies of the Koran and texts containing decorative Arabic script.

Not quite as good for merchandise, but even more picturesque, is the **Egyptian Spice Bazaar** bordering the Golden Horn. Here you can buy a fragrant variety of spices, tapes of Turkish music, as well as henna, cheeses and dried fruits.

TRANSPORT CLASH

Istanbul's major new transport link, the Marmaray – an undersea rail tunnel to link the Asian and European halves of the city – has been badly delayed, first by the discovery of the city's Byzantine port, an archaeological treasure trove which has turned up over 30 ancient ships, and, more recently, the oldest evidence of habitation in the city so far discovered, dating back to 6,000BC. At the time of this update, the projected date for the opening is late 2013 (http://marmaray.com).

THE DEATH OF A GREAT LEADER

The room in the Dolmabahçe Palace where Atatürk died on 10 November 1938 is of great national significance to the Turkish people. All clocks in the palace are kept at 09:05, the time at which Atatürk passed away. Every 10 November the entire nation comes to a halt (literally), and observes a two-minute silence, starting at 09:05 precisely (www.millisaraylar.gov.tr/portalmain-en/default.aspx).

▲ *Above: The ancient art of belly dancing is an Ottoman legacy.*
▶ *Opposite: Burgaz Ada, one of the Princes' Islands in the Sea of Marmara.*

In recent years, Istanbul has blossomed as an international shoppers' paradise. In addition to the hugely atmospheric bazaars, fashionistas flock to the trendy boutiques that line Istiklâl Caddesi in Beyoğlu and Bagdat Caddesi on the Asian shore, while designer showrooms from all corners of the globe cluster into high-end department stores, the wealthy residential suburbs of Nisantasi and Levent, and vast shopping malls. Zeytinburnu, halfway to the airport, has a number of excellent leather outlet stores.

You'll either love **Turkish music** or loathe it. Very few Turkish singers have made it internationally, as Tarkan did a few years ago, but others such as Murat Boz have a huge local following. A large proportion of the cassettes and CDs that are offered for sale are not originals and, therefore, inexpensive.

The City at Night **

Istanbul is very much a night-time city and restaurants and clubs hum with activity in the evening. If you wish to enjoy a night out at a club where you can see exotic **belly dancing**, try Kervansaray Nightclub close to the Hilton at 30 Cumhuriyet Caddesi, tel: 212 247 1630; Orient House, Tiyatro Caddesi 27, Beyazit, tel: 212 517 6163; or the Galata Tower, tel: 212 293 8180. All include dinner and a floor show, but none are cheap.

Beyoğlu has its down side but it is without doubt the focal point of serious club life for Istanbul's young and restless, and gay. As local musicians start playing their own material instead of western covers, venues such as Peyote (Kameriye Sokak 4, Balikpazari, tel: 212 251 4398) and Dogzstar (Kartal Sokak 3 Kat:3, Galatasaray, tel: 212 244 9147) have given Turkish indie-rockers a platform to experiment. Meantime, the beautiful people are still likely to be found in sleek rooftop cocktail bars or on the waterfront in Ortaköy, dancing till dawn at vast clubs such as Reina, tel: 212 259 5919, Club Crystal, tel: 212 261 1988 and Angelique, tel: 212 327 2844, or at exclusive SuAda, which has its own Bosphorus island, tel: 212 263 73 00. Live jazz erupts at Babylon, just off Asmalı Mescit Sokak, tel: 212 292 7368. The **Istanbul Jazz Festival** is one of the highlights of the year.

Bath Time

One of the best ways to relax in Turkey is to go for a Turkish bath – a combination swim, steam and massage, all at an affordable price. Three of Turkey's finest historic bathhouses are in the Old City – the Cagalaoğlu Hamami, Prof. Kazim Ismail Gürkan Cad 3; the Çemberlitas Hamami, Vezhirhan Cad; and the Süleymaniye Hamami, Mimar Sinan Cad. 20. (*See also* panel, page 54.)

For many of the locals, a night on the town often includes a visit to one of the many *gazinos*. These are old-style Turkish clubs, where singers, agile oriental dancers and jugglers entertain the customers. Drinks and *meze* are served. The backstreets of Beyoğlu, off Istiklâl Caddesi, are sleazy. Resist invitations by locals to accompany them to bars here. You will be paying and this is a variation on extortion. There are more enjoyable ways to savour the nightlife in Istanbul.

The younger crowd tend to opt for 'cooler' options such as the **Chianti Café-Pub**, Balo Sokak 31/2, Istiklâl Caddesi, Beyoğlu; **Badehane**, General Yazgan Sokak 5, Tünel; or the **Jazz Café**, Hasnün Galip Sokak 20, off Büyükparmakkapi Sokak, Beyoğlu.

For a truly romantic evening, try a **dinner cruise** on the Bosphorus (details in the lobbies of most hotels).

The huge **Atatürk Kültür Merkezi** (Taksim Square) is due to reopen in late 2013 after a major renovation, providing a central home for classical music, opera and dance which are currently spread across the city.

Nightlife in Istanbul is lively but it comes into its own for the **Istanbul International Festival** (end of June to mid-July, www.iksv.org) which specializes in exhibitions and performances by leading Turkish and international performing artists.

The Asian Shore

Üsküdar has some fine mosques, the imposing Haydarpaşa Station, the British War Cemetery, and the Selimiye Barracks, where Florence Nightingale had her Crimean Hospital; there's still a small museum. Nearby Kadiköy and Moda are popular areas with some fine restaurants and an antique tram. Museums on the Asian shore include the Toy Museum, Göztepe (www.istanbuloyuncakmuzesi.com); the Sabri Artam Foundation Automobile Museum (Nato Yolu Bosna Boulevard No. 104, Çengelköy); and the TÜRVAK Cinema and TV Museum (Ekinciler Caddesi No. 4, Kavacik, Beykoz).

OUTSIDE THE CITY CENTRE

Of the nine islands in the **Princes' Islands**, four are inhabited and many well-off Istanbulites retreat here for the summer months. The city centre is still close enough for corporate commuters. The islands are tranquil, with pine trees and beautiful villas. Vehicular traffic is forbidden. Sea buses and ferries are the best way to access the islands.

Polonezköy was a haven for Polish refugees in 1842 and its population is descended from them. It is green and tranquil with excellent pathways for walking. Weekends are crowded, as it is only a stone's throw from Istanbul proper. There are several outstanding restaurants here.

Best Times to Visit

Spring (Apr–Jun) and **autumn** (Sep–Oct) are the most temperate months. Summers can be steamy hot and winters wet and damp. Istanbul frequently has snow and frost in winter.

Getting There

Havaş, Turkish Airlines' ground service operator, runs regular buses to both airports from the north side of Taksim Square and the Old City (45 mins to International; 1hr 15 mins to Sabiha Gokcen). Istanbul International is on the metro. There are plenty of taxis and hotel shuttles at International; taxis are an expensive option from Sabiha Gokcen.

Getting Around

Istanbul has a rapidly growing and increasingly sophisticated public transport network with a metro system on both sides of the Bosphorus (shortly to be linked by tunnel and bridge), a modern tram line running from the airport through Sultanahmet along the Bosphorus, suburban trains, funiculars, buses and a large fleet of efficient and affordable yellow taxis. Meantime, commuter ferries ply the Bosphorus and Marmara Sea between Karaköy, Eminönü and Ataköy on the European side and Kadiköy and Bostancı on the Asian side. Payment for all public transport is via an electronic smartcard, the Istanbulkart. There are two antique trams – on Istiklal Caddesi in Beyoğlu and in Moda, on the Asian shore.

Where to Stay

Luxury

Çirağan Palace Hotel Kempinski, Çirağan Caddesi, Beşiktaş, tel: 212 326 4646, www.kempinski-istanbul.com Fabulous Ottoman palace on the Bosphorus with superb views and restaurants. A touch of royal luxury.

Grand Hyatt, Taşkıyla Caddesi, Taksim, tel: 212 368 1234, www.istanbul.grand.hyatt.com World-class hotel with charming Turkish touches. Excellent business centre.

Sumahan on the Water, Kuleli Caddesi 51, Çengelköy, tel: 216 422 8000, www.sumahan.com A chic architect-designed boutique hotel on the Asian shore with fabulous views and a wonderful seafood restaurant.

Conrad Istanbul, Barbaros Bulvarı, Beşiktaş, tel: 212 310 2525, www.conradhotels.com A huge modern hotel with Bosphorous views, fine restaurants and pools.

Pera Palas, Meşrütiyet Caddesi 98, Tepebaşı, tel: 212 222 8090, www.jumeirah.com The old Orient Express railway hotel. Everyone from Agatha Christie to Trotsky stayed here. A recent facelift has restored this grandest of old ladies to her true glory.

Four Seasons Hotel, Tevkifhane Sok 1, Sultanahmet, tel: 212 402 3000, www.fourseasons.com/istanbul A beautifully restored Ottoman prison with one of the city's best restaurants.

Budget

Hotel Nomade, Divanyolu, Ticarethane Sokak 15, Sultanahmet, tel: 212 513 8172, www.hotelnomade.com Comfortable small French-run hotel with rooftop terrace, and a bistro across the street.

Orient Hostel International, Yeni Akbiyik Caddesi 13, Sultanahmet, tel: 212 517 9493, www.orienthostel.com This is an excellent cheap hostel with de luxe rooms, doubles and dorms. There's a restaurant and bar (with belly dancing and live music), internet access, luggage storage and an onsite travel agency.

Naz Wooden House Inn, Yeni Akbiyik Degirmeni Sokak 7, Sultanahmet, tel: 212 516 7130, www.nazwoodenhouseinn.com Wooden house built on the remains of an 8th-century Byzantine building. Seven comfortable rooms with private bath, air conditioning, central heating, TV. Fine views.

Special Hotels

These restored period buildings are usually three- or four-star standard and mid-range in price. As most are small and very popular, they should be booked in advance.

Ottoman Hotel Imperial, Caferiye Sokak No 6/1, 34400 Sultanahmet, tel: 212 513 6150/1, www.ottomanhotelimperial.com 19th-century school and hospital beautifully transformed into a luxurious hotel with a traditional Ottoman dining room.

Neorion Hotel, Orhaniye Street No 14, 34110 Sirkeci, tel: 212 527 9090, www.neorionhotel.com 58-room boutique hotel with spa that is attracting rave reviews and awards for its friendly efficient service.
Empress Zoë, Akbıyık Cad, Adliya Sokak 10, Sultanahmet, tel: 212 518 4360, www.emzoe.com Lovingly restored with garden, Bosphorus and resident ruins; steep spiral staircase; American-owned.
Ibrahim Paşa, Terzihane Sokak 5, Sultanahmet, tel: 212 518 0394, www.ibrahimpasha.com A beautiful small hotel close to the Blue Mosque.

Where to Eat

Kebap houses, buffets (*büfe*) and fast-food joints can supply cheap meals on the run. Most of the listed restaurants are quite expensive but represent good Turkish food.
Areas to aim for include the fishermen's quarter of Kumkapi, behind Sultanahmet; Istiklal Caddesi and its side alleys in the new town, particularly Çicek Passage and Nevizade Sokak, which are crammed with restaurants.
Konyali, Topkapı Palace Sultanahmet, tel: 212 513 9696, www.konyalilokantasi.com In the palace grounds, this restaurant serves Ottoman cuisine. Lunch only, but there is another branch in Kanyon shopping centre.
Türkistan Aşevi, Tavukhane Sokak 36, Sultanahmet, tel: 212 638 6525, www.turkistanasevi.com A jolly Anatolian café-restaurant overlooking the Hippodrome, open all day, offering everything from a cup of coffee to full meals. No alcohol.
Balıkcı Sabahattin, Seyit Hasankuyu Sokak 50, off Cankurtaran Caddesi, Sultanahmet, tel: 212 458 1824, www.balikcisabahattin.com Wonderful fish restaurant, with pavement terrace and gypsy music.
Leb-i-Derya, Kumbaraci Yokusu 115/7, Tünel, tel: 212 293 4989, www.lebiderya.com This is one of the city's trendiest restaurants. The food is fabulous and the terrace has fine views. Book ahead. Live music late night.
Feriye Lokantasi, Çirağan Caddesi 40, Ortaköy, tel: 212 227 2216/7, www.feriye.com An excellent grill on the Bosphorus that is hugely popular year round, especially for Sunday brunch. Be sure to book ahead.
Asitane, Kariye Hotel, Kariye Camii Sokak 18, Edirnekapı, tel: 212 534 8414, www.asitanerestaurant.com Ottoman court cuisine served in a leafy courtyard next to the Kariye Monastery. Worth the detour for an imperial feast.

Tours and Excursions

The most reliable agents include the following:
Arttours, Nazmi Akbaci Ticaret Merkezi 68, 34396 Maslak, tel: 212 346 4266, www.arttours.com
Plan Tours, Cumhuriyet Cad. 83/1, Elmadağ, tel: 212 234 7777, www.plantours.com
City Sightseeing, tel: 212 458 1800, www.city-sightseeing.com operate a hop-on, hop-off bus tour around key sights.
American Express, Teşvikiye, tel: 212 283 2201.
Visa, Eurocard and MasterCard, Levent, tel: 212 225 0080.
The Touring and Automobile Club of Turkey (TTOK), Oto Sanayi Sitesi yanı 4, Levent, tel: 212 282 8140, www.turing.org.tr/eng/tarihcemiz.asp They offer motoring information as well as a vehicle rescue service.

Useful Contacts

Tourist offices: The main office is in Sultanahmet, tel: 212 518 1802. There are also information points at both airports, both stations, the main ferry terminals in Beyazit, Taksim and at several other points in the city. Visit the website: http://english.istanbul.com

ISTANBUL	J	F	M	A	M	J	J	A	S	O	N	D
AVERAGE TEMP. °F	46	47	51	60	69	77	82	82	76	68	59	51
AVERAGE TEMP. °C	8	9	11	16	21	25	28	28	24	20	15	11
RAINFALL in	4	4	3	2	2	1	1	1	2	3	4	5
RAINFALL mm	109	92	72	46	38	34	34	30	58	81	103	119
DAYS OF RAINFALL	18	14	14	9	8	6	4	4	7	11	14	18

3
Around the Sea of Marmara

The northwestern part of the country, including the **Sea of Marmara** and the European plains, is often overlooked in favour of more glamorous spots, yet it contains a wider display of Ottoman sights than almost anywhere else in Turkey and should not be missed.

This region witnessed the youth of the Ottoman Empire, whose first capital was at **Bursa**, just south of the Sea of Marmara. **Edirne**, up near the Greek border, was also a capital of the Ottoman Empire. In the 15th century it was renowned throughout the Middle East for its hundreds of splendid mosques and fountains, rivalled only by Baghdad.

At the western end of the Sea of Marmara are the **Dardanelles**, a narrow strip of water that has been of great strategic importance since ancient times. The northern shore of the Dardanelles is formed by the **Gallipoli Peninsula** (*Gelibolu*), scene of one of the most disastrous campaigns of World War I. The battlefields here remain largely undisturbed, and many a moving relic from the campaign is on view in the museum at **Çanakkale**.

The Sea of Marmara also contains some delightful, small islands, which are well worth visiting for their quaint fishing villages and lovely beaches. They can be reached by ferry from Erdek, on the edge of the **Kapıdağı Peninsula**. Another neglected spot is the historic walled town of **Iznik**, where artists produced the beautiful tiles that today adorn many of the finest mosques throughout Turkey.

Don't Miss

***** **Gallipoli Peninsula:** site of the ill-fated Gallipoli Campaign of World War I.
***** **Edirne:** its mosques are among the finest in Turkey.
**** **Marmara Islands:** delightful, small islands with fishing villages and beaches, very popular with Turkish holiday-makers.
**** **Bursa:** first capital of the Ottoman Empire, renowned for its mosques and baths.
* **Uludağ:** one of Turkey's winter ski resorts, also good for summer hiking.

◀ *Opposite: The marvellous dome and decorated ceiling of Edirne's impressive Selimiye Camii mosque.*

CLIMATE

Northwestern Turkey has a more **moderate** climate than the rest of the country. In winter it's often wet and cold, average temperatures sinking to around 8°C (46°F). It warms up a bit in spring, with sunny days and occasional rain. **Summer** tends to be dry and warm, never extremely hot. Average temperatures seldom exceed 30°C (86°F), except during the occasional unpredictable heatwave. **Autumn** often has long sunny spells, with only occasional rain, until the weather finally breaks around late October.

EDIRNE

If you drive west from Istanbul, out across the rolling plains of European Turkey for approximately 225km (140 miles), you will see the famous skyline of Edirne, with its distinctive domes and minarets rising dramatically against the horizon.

Edirne lies on the **Meriç River**, quite close to the Greek border. This ancient city was once proud **Adrianople**, capital of **Thrace**, the province which covered European Turkey, northern Greece and part of southern Bulgaria. It was founded by the ancient Romans in the 2nd century AD, and named after the **Emperor Hadrian**. Sultan Murat captured the city in 1361, and for almost a century it remained the capital of the steadily expanding Ottoman Empire. During the 15th century, Süleyman the Magnificent made Edirne his summer capital, and it became one of the greatest cities in the Middle East, rivalling beautiful and famous Baghdad in its splendour, with almost 300 mosques and 100 public fountains.

Selimiye Camii ★★

Many of the old mosques are still standing. The finest is the Selimiye Camii, built in the 16th century by a then aged **Mimar Sinan**, greatest mosque architect of all time, who considered this his masterpiece. It was built for **Selim the Grim**, and according to local legend has 999 windows, because Selim didn't want to tempt fate by having a thousand. Its four minarets are over 70m (230ft) high; only those in Mecca are higher.

Inside, the superb high dome is even wider than that of Aya Sofya in Istanbul. Its surface is inscribed with delicate calligraphy, offering prayers to Allah. The sultan's lodge is probably the only one in Turkey with a window opening towards Mecca.

◀ *Left: Musicians look on as eager competitors line up for the Kırkpınar Oil Wrestling Championships.*

◀◀ *Opposite: Edirne used to be one of the greatest cities in the Middle East; it's still a lively centre.*

Worth a visit is the **Museum of Turkish and Islamic Arts**, east of the Selimiye Camii. It has a range of historic exhibits, including some excellent ceramic tiles and portraits of previous Kırkpınar (oil wrestling) champions.

The Old Town ★

Across **Dilaver Bey** (central park) from the Selimiye Camii you come to the **Bedesten**, one of the oldest covered markets in Turkey, selling mostly household goods. Its structure consists of over a dozen vaulted chambers, which do wonders for amplifying the hubbub of the traders below. It was created to fund the **Eski Camii** (1403–15) and was at one stage so wealthy that it required 60 night watchmen. The caravanserai stayed in by the traders is still a hotel. Just west of the Bedesten lies the ancient **Kale Içı** quarter, its grid-patterned streets and old, terraced houses dating from Byzantine times. The Karaağaç area is filled with old houses, small cafés and tea shops, and is a lively place for an evening stroll.

Edirne Saray ★

Follow the walk east along the river to **Sarayiçi**, the island supporting the rather disappointing ruins of the Sultan's Palace, which centuries ago rivalled the Topkapı in Istanbul. Nearby is the stadium where the **Kırkpınar** Championships are held. Across the Tunça River, the **Beyazit Külliyesi** is an extraordinary 15th-century mental hospital, now home to a bizarre museum of health.

Oil Wrestling

Edirne is famous as the venue for the Kırkpınar Wrestling Championships held annually in late June to early July, depending on Ramazan. Based on wrestling contests originally designed as military training and fought to the death, contestants cover their bodies from head to foot in olive oil, and wear hand-crafted leather pants (*kıspet*). The championships are judged according to weight groups. The loser is the first contestant to collapse or be pinned to the ground. Thousands of contestants come from all over Turkey, and the winner achieves great prestige for his region or village.

▲ *Above: The toll of war – World War I gravestones at Gallipoli.*

GALLIPOLI PENINSULA

Çanakkale ★

About 190km (120 miles) south of Edirne, down the E87, you come to Çanakkale. This somewhat drab but strategically placed town is situated at the entrance to the Dardanelles.

Çanakkale makes an ideal base for visiting the Gallipoli battlefields on the **Gelibolu Peninsula** (across the Dardanelles by ferry). The local **Army and Navy Museum** contains a great number of fascinating relics from the historical campaign, including the pocket watch which miraculously saved Atatürk's life by stopping a bullet.

Also of interest, the **Archaeological Museum** displays finds unearthed at Ancient Troy, 27km (17 miles) away. Unfortunately this doesn't include the major discoveries, which are housed either in the national museums or in Germany. To make up for this, the museum has a small but superb collection of ancient coins, ranging from primitive pre-Hellenic groats to magnificent Ottoman sovereigns. Open Tue–Sat 08:30–12:00 and 13:00–17:30.

The Legend of Hero and Leander

In ancient times the Dardanelles, known then as the Hellespont, was the site of one of the most romantic of Ancient Greek legends. Each night Leander would swim across this treacherous strait for a tryst with his lover, the priestess Hero. She would always light a lantern in her tower to guide him. One night a storm blew out the lantern, and before Hero could relight it, Leander lost his way and was drowned. When his body was discovered the next morning, an anguished Hero flung herself into the waves to be reunited with her dead lover.

Gökçeada ★

This is the ancient *Imbros* mentioned by **Homer** and was used as the Allied HQ during the Gallipoli campaign. Ferries to the island run on a regular basis from Çanakkale. On Gökçeada you can explore the island's 15th-century castle ruin and some fine but remote beaches.

The World War I Battlefields ★★★

In 1915 **Winston Churchill** hatched a daring plan to resupply the ailing Russian forces and knock Turkey out of the war. The British and French fleets were to force their way up the Dardanelles and bombard Istanbul until the Turks capitulated, but the plan turned into a fiasco. Most of the Allied warships were stopped by the batteries guarding the entrance to the **Dardanelles** at Çanakkale; the few that managed to battle past, fell victim to mines. Churchill decided to try a different tack: the Allies would invade the Gallipoli Peninsula and take the Dardanelles.

On 25 April 1915, British, French and ANZAC (Australia and New Zealand Army Corps) troops invaded. The beaches were narrow, bordered by steeply rising terrain – and the Turks were waiting. A narrow beachhead was established and remained under constant bombardment from the Turks, but the Allies dug in. Their **trenches,** very often only 20m (65ft) from the Turkish lines, are still visible amid the fragrant pines.

The Allies persisted for over eight months, by which time around 160,000 Allies and 86,000 Turks lay dead. The resistance, originally led by a German general, was handed to young Lt-Col Mustafa Kemal, whose ruthless brilliance won the day and turned him into a national hero. In January 1916, the Allies finally withdrew, having achieved absolutely nothing. Churchill was forced to resign in disgrace.

Begin your tour of the battlefields at the **Kabatepe Military Museum**, with its stirring exhibit of photos and relics from the campaign. Some 30 **cemeteries** serve as a reminder of the atrocities of war. You can also visit the beaches and trenches, where poignant remains of the war linger on in the form of rusted bully-beef tins and spent bullets.

The best, most informative way to take in the sights is to join one of the day-long **tours** which start from Çanakkale. These are conducted by guides whose intimate knowledge of the battlefields and the surrounding area brings history to life.

ANZAC Day

The Gallipoli Campaign saw some exceptionally brave fighting by the Australians and New Zealanders who made up the **ANZAC** troops. Many thousands of them lost their lives here. ANZAC Day is a public holiday in both **Australia** and **New Zealand** to commemorate the fallen in both World Wars. It is held on 25 April, the day of the first Gallipoli landings. A self-guided tour of the peninsula is available, with plaques set up at key sites by the Anzacs, and a guidebook is available from the local museums. Allow a full day to do the whole route.

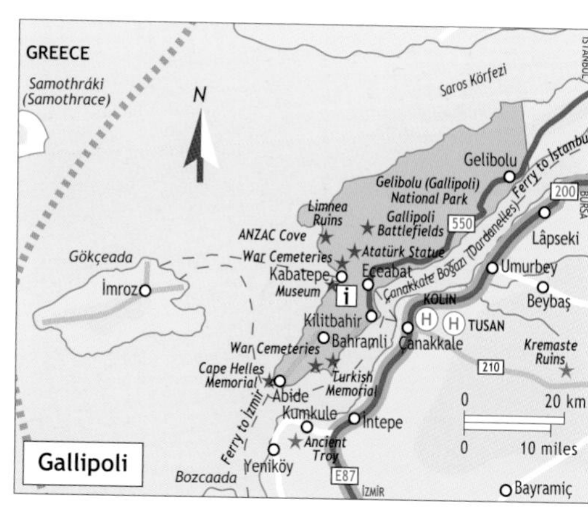

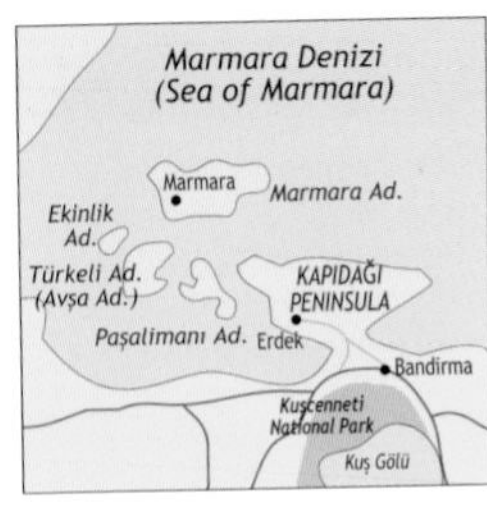

MARMARA ISLANDS

These are the small, pleasant islands which lie at the southwestern end of the Sea of Marmara. They can be reached by regular **ferry services** from **Tekirdağ** (on the north coast) and **Erdek,** on the south coast, and also by direct ferry access from **Istanbul** (summer months only). There are over half a dozen islands, but only the four largest ones are permanently inhabited. The Marmara Islands are very popular with Turkish tourists during the **summer**, but they seldom become overrun, except during weekends at the height of the season.

Marmara Island is the largest of the group and has a length of about 16km (10 miles). Some 2500 years ago this was a flourishing colony of the Ionian-Greek city of Miletus, whose ruins lie 300km (190 miles) away on the southwestern coast of mainland Turkey. Marmara Island was famous for its marble (*marmara* is Greek for marble, hence the colony's name) and there is still a mine in the north of the island. The main coastal village, also called Marmara, has steep, picturesque streets, and there are several good beaches and swimming coves along the coast.

Avşa Island, which lies to the southwest, also has some very fine beaches and is famous for its wine. **Paşalimanı** is more wooded and remote, and **Ekinlik** is even more remote, with just one tiny village.

Turkish Baths

On entering the baths you divest yourself of your clothes in a cubicle and proceed to the steaming room, clad in a towel. Here you relax on a large, hot, circular stone platform. This process opens the pores, and is extremely tranquilizing and soothing. Here you can also subject yourself to a vigorous traditional massage. Afterwards you enter the warming and cooling rooms, where you douse yourself alternately with hot and cold water, which is both relaxing and exhilarating. Many spend hours in the *hamam*, taking beer or tea, or even having a snooze. Afterwards you will feel wonderfully clean and revitalized. A visit to the baths costs little and is a quintessentially Turkish experience.

▶▶ *Opposite: The presence of Sultan Mehmet I is still felt in Bursa, not least in his Green Mausoleum.*

▶ *Right: Marmara Island can be a haven of tranquility, though in summer it receives plenty of visitors.*

BURSA

The sprawling city of Bursa lies just 20km (12½ miles) inland, at the southeastern end of the Sea of Marmara. Nowadays it is renowned mainly for producing cars and textiles including wonderful and very affordable silk. Yet many remains of its long illustrious past are preserved.

The site of Bursa is said to have been chosen in the 3rd century BC by **Hannibal**, the famous Carthaginian general. Later it was occupied by the **Romans**, and then by the **Crusaders**. Finally, in 1326 it was taken by the Turks and became the first capital of the expanding Ottoman Empire. Ever since then, Bursa has been held in particular affection.

Bursa **knives** are renowned throughout Turkey and are on sale all over the city. Bursa is also renowned for its thermal springs, the most famous of which are the **Yeni Kaplıca**, which were built nearly 500 years ago on a site dating back to Roman times.

Yeşil Camii ★★

The town of Bursa has several superb mosques, the finest of which is the **Green Mosque** (Yeşil Camii), built in the early 15th century by Sultan Mehmet I who so loved it that he lived in it. Opposite, you can see the sultan's magnificent tomb, the **Green Mausoleum**. Of particular interest is the fine marble carving around the main door. This was the first mosque to reflect a

Exchanging Populations

The Marmara islands and their fishing villages look very Greek. This is not surprising, for they were inhabited by Greeks until early this century. Then relations between Greece and Turkey became so bad that the whole Greek population of Turkey was shipped back to Greece, in exchange for as many Turks living in Greece. Altogether some 1.5 million people were moved, many of whom had never before set foot in their 'native' land. On some maps you will still see the old Greek names for these islands. Marmara was called Elafonissos, Avşa was Ophioussa, and Paşalimanı was known as Haloni.

Mustafa Kemal

The Turkish troops who fought at Gallipoli were composed largely of ill-trained and ill-equipped peasant recruits. They were led by Lt-Col Mustafa Kemal, undoubtedly Turkey's greatest military genius. Kemal believed in inspiring his troops with acts of personal bravery, often directing his men in full view of enemy guns. Later Mustafa Kemal went on to become the first president of modern Turkey, adopting the name Atatürk, Father of the Turks.

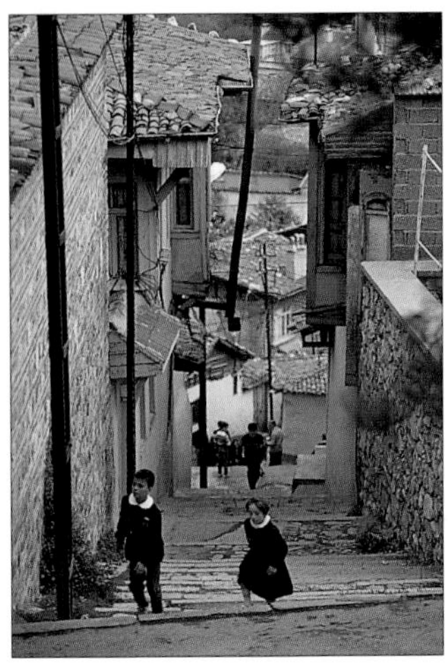

▲ *Above: Picturesque street in an old quarter of Bursa.*
▶ *Opposite: Iznik is known for its blue-green tiles.*

truly Turkish style. Previous builders had followed Persian designs, but here we see evolving the style which was to achieve its final glory in the works of Sinan and the great mosques of Istanbul.

Ulu Camii ★★

Another mosque that shouldn't be missed is the Ulu Camii, which stands in the town centre and dates from the reign of **Sultan Yıldırım Beyazıt I** in the late 14th century. It has no less than 20 domes, and the interior contains a pleasant pool and some fine woodwork. This mosque is known especially for its *mihrab* (carved prayer niche indicating the direction of Mecca). Next door, the old silk market, the **Koza Han**, is still filled with silk shops – an essential shopping stop.

The city also has several excellent museums, including an archaeological museum and a number of restored merchants' houses in the suburb of Muradiye (the Museum of 17th-century Ottoman Houses, the 19th-century Hüsnü Züber House Museum and the Mudanya Mütareke House Museum where the ceasefire that ended the Turko-Greek war of 1923 was signed).

Iznik's Moments of Greatness

In AD325 Iznik was the site of the first **Ecumenical Council.** Here, elders of the Christian Church decided upon the **Nicaean Creed** which outlined the fundamental tenets of Christian belief. The second council was also held here, 400 years later, under the Byzantine **Empress Irene**. This time rituals were formalized into the structure that the Greek church still adheres to today. After the sacking of Constantinople in 1204, Iznik briefly became the capital of the Byzantine Empire.

Çekirge ★

A suburb of Bursa en route to Uludağ, Çekirge is known for its mineral and thermal baths. It is ideal if you want to get away from the city centre.

Of particular interest here is the **Karagöz Theatre and Museum**, Çekirge Caddesiz, with displays and performances of Karagöz shadow puppet plays. These are said to have originated in Bursa, and once appeared in travelling shows throughout the Ottoman Empire. Indeed, they remained popular in the Balkans until 50 years ago.

The origin of these plays, which are reminiscent of the British 'Punch and Judy' shows, has its own legend. According to this tale, comical Karagöz and his partner, Hacıvat, fell foul of Sultan Orhan, because they distracted fellow workers building the **Orhan Gazi Camii** with their antics. In anger, he ordered to have them beheaded, but later came to miss the funny pair and promptly ordered their return as shadow characters, thus ensuring their immortality.

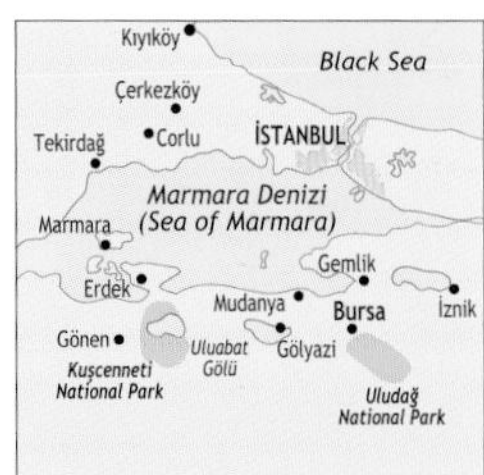

Uludağ ★

This mountain, at the centre of a **national park** just to the south of Bursa, provides a spectacular backdrop to the city and is one of its main attractions. Uludağ rises to over 2500m (8200ft) and for much of the year is covered in snow. In winter there is a **ski resort** near the top. In summer you can go **hiking** along well-marked trails in the woods, or up to the lakes near the summit. The mountain can be reached from **Teferüç** in south Bursa, where there is a **cable car** which takes you up to over 1600m (5200ft).

Bursa Silk

In late Roman times, silk was an expensive luxury. It had to be imported all the way from **China** along the **Silk Road**, and the Chinese jealously guarded the secret of making silk. Eventually, a group of Nestorians succeeded in smuggling out **silk worms** in hollow canes. The caterpillars were brought to Bursa, which established itself as the new centre of the silk trade.

Uluabat Gölü ★

About 40km (25 miles) west of Bursa, off the main road to **Bandırma**, lies the Lake of Uluabat. Around it there are several picturesque Ottoman villages, like the little fishing village of **Gölyazı** at the eastern end of the lake.

IZNIK

This market town, lying approximately 80km (50 miles) northeast of Bursa on the shore of the scenic **Lake Iznik**, is surrounded by ancient city walls. The ruined old church is renowned for its splendid frescoes and mosaics which date from Byzantine times. The main mosque, Yeşil Camii, dates from the late 15th century.

Opposite Yeşil Camii, the **Iznik Museum** contains some excellent examples of the blue-green **tiles** for which this town was once famous (*see* panel, page 36).

The city itself was probably founded around 3000 years ago. It was originally known as Nicaea, and it was here that Christian belief was formalized in AD325 in the Nicene Creed.

AROUND THE SEA OF MARMARA AT A GLANCE

Best Times to Visit

This region can be cold and wet in **winter**, but there is good **skiing** (by Turkish standards) on the slopes of Uludağ, just south of Bursa. Spring is still cool, but the flowers are superb. Summer can be hot at midday, and the beaches beckon most. **Autumn** is an excellent time to visit, with long **sunny** days.

Getting There

There are internal flights from Istanbul to Bursa. Ferries run from Istanbul to the Marmara Islands in summer and to Yalova on the south shore year-round. There are regular bus and dolmuş services from Istanbul to Edirne, Çanakkale and Iznik. Istanbul is also linked to Edirne by rail.

Getting Around

The main towns and sights in this region are connected by regular bus and dolmuş services, with the exception of the Marmara Islands, These are linked by ferry services from Erdek on the Kapıdağ Peninsula. There is also a ferry across the Dardanelles from Çanakkale to Eceabat. All these ferries take cars.

Where to Stay

Bursa

Luxury

Çelik Palas Oteli Swissôtel, Çekirge Caddesi 79, tel: 224 233 3800, www.celikpalasotel.com Bursa's premier hotel with thermal baths and hamam. Excellent bars and good restaurant.

Mid-range

Ağaoğlu My Resort Hotel, Uludağ, tel: 224 285 2001, http://en.agaoglumyresort.com.tr One of the best of the ski resorts in the mountains above the city, also open in summer for those who want to walk or just get away from the concrete.

Kitap Evi, Kavaklı Mah. Burç üstü No 21, 16040 Tophane, tel: 224 225 41 60, www.kitapevi.com.tr A former bookstore and café, now a special hotel with individually designed rooms and one of the best restaurants in town.

Otantik Club Hotel, Botanik Parkı Soğanlı, tel: 224 211 3280, www.otantikclubhotel.com Comfortable small hotel near airport, with good facilities including indoor and outdoor pools, *hamam*, full fitness centre and garden.

Safran Hotel, Ortapazar Caddesi, Arka Sokak 4, Tophane, tel: 224 224 7216, fax: 224 224 7219, www.safranotel.com Comfortable restored house in a quiet old town street. Wooden architecture, modern amenities and a good restaurant.

Çanakkale

Mid-range

Anzac Hotel, Saat Kulesi Meydanı 8, tel: 286 217 7777, www.anzachotel.com Recently overhauled, this boutique hotel is themed around the local sights, including Gallipoli and Troy. The rooms are comfortable, and the roof bar is a great place on summer evenings.

Kolin Hotel, Kepez 17100 Çanakkale, tel: 286 218 0808, www.kolinhotel.com Just outside the centre, overlooking the Dardanelles, this huge five-star resort offers everything from beach and pool to massage and entertainment.

Hotel Limani, Yalı cad. No 12, Çanakkale 17100, tel: 286 217 2908, www.hotellimani.com Friendly small family-run hotel near the ferry port in the town centre. Convenient, comfortable and helpful.

Edirne

Mid-range

Rys Hotel, 1 Murat Mah. Talatpasa Cad. No 82, Merkez, Edirne 22030, tel: 532 111 1797, www.ryshotel.com This new 4-star boutique design hotel with a café-bar and spa has finally brought a small amount of chic to Edirne.

Hotel Rüstem Pasa Kervansaray, Iki Kapılı Han Caddesi 57, Sabuni Mahallesi, tel: 284 212 6119, fax: 284 212 0462, www.edirnekervansarayhotel.com Beautifully restored if somewhat spartan16th-century inn, designed by master architect, Sinan. Pleasantly cool in summer; freezing in winter.

Where to Eat

Bursa

Bursa has relatively few really outstanding restaurants. There are, however, many modest lokantas and kebap places and several attractive restaurants in the Kulturpark.

Iskender, Heykel, tel: 224 444 1618, www.iskender.

com.tr Original home of Turkey's famous Iskender kebab (doner smothered with tomato-garlic sauce, butter and yoghurt). This is all they serve. Be prepared to queue.

Çanakkale
Yalova, Liman Caddesi, tel: 286 217 1045, www.yalovarestaurant.com Excellent seafood restaurant near ferry port.

Edirne
Köfteci Hocaoğlu, Saraçlar Caddesi 73, Zindanaltı, tel: 284 214 7300. Cheap, clean and cheerful town centre local, specializing in good meatballs.

The real local speciality in Edirne is fried liver. Look for speciality *cigerci restorans*.

Lalezar Restaurant, Karaağaç Yolu, tel: 284 213 0600. Attractive restaurant just out of town, with good traditional Turkish food, moderate prices and a riverfront terrace. There are several other places nearby if this one is full.

Gelibolu
Gelibolu Restoran, on the harbour. Wonderful harbour views, ultra-fresh fish, beautifully prepared, friendly service and reasonable prices.

Tours and Excursions

Every tour operator and travel agent in Istanbul, Marmara and the north Aegean will offer tours of the Gallipoli peninsula. Amongst the best are those run by Hassle Free Travel, who also own the Anzac House (*see* Hotels), from where you can book. In Bursa a bus service links all the main tourist sights in town. Its route starts at the Emir Sultan Cami at the eastern end of town, and ends at the baths in Çekirge suburb. There are no tours as such of the **Marmara Islands**. However, there are plenty of ferries from the harbour in Erdek and it is easy to set up your own trip.

Skiing at Uludağ:
Though the standard of skiing in Turkey is not really comparable to that in the Alpine areas, a relaxing weekend at Uludağ makes for a refreshing break, and it is also a convenient travelling distance from Istanbul. All the necessary skiing equipment can be hired at the local hotels, of which there were 27 at the last count, along with the required chalets and apartments. You could also stay in **Bursa** and head to the slopes for the day. The skiing is mainly intermediate level, with a chaotic system of 14 ski lifts which all seem to need different passes. The main season lasts from January to March.

Shopping

The heart of Turkey's textile industry is in Bursa, which is the ideal place to buy top-quality silk, towels, bathrobes and home furnishing items. Many factories, such as Özdilek, have outlet stores along the Yalova Road. An entertaining way of shopping is in the Koza Han, where dozens of small shops draped in silk vie for trade.

Useful Contacts

Tourism Information Offices:
Bursa: Ulucami Parkı Orhangazi Alt Geçidi 1 Heykel, tel: 224 220 1848.
Çanakkale: next to harbour, tel/fax: 286 217 1187.
Iznik: Kılıçarslan Caddesi, Belediye Hizmet Binası, tel: 224 757 1454.
Edirne: Hükümet Caddesi 17/A, tel: 284 225 3029.
Travel Agents:
Trooper Tours, Hocapasa Mah. Tayahatun Sok. Sukran Han No 3, Kat 3, Sirkeci, Istanbul 34112, tel: 212 520 0434 , www.troopertours.com Specialist day and weekend tours to Gallipoli from Istanbul.
Turkish Airlines, 24-hour central reservations, tel: 212 444 0849, www.thy.com.tr

BURSA	J	F	M	A	M	J	J	A	S	O	N	D
AVERAGE TEMP. °F	47	48	51	60	69	78	81	81	76	69	60	52
AVERAGE TEMP. °C	9	9	11	17	22	24	27	27	23	22	17	11
RAINFALL in	4	4	3	2	2	1	1	1	2	3	4	5
RAINFALL mm	102	90	71	41	38	35	34	31	55	80	103	120
DAYS OF RAINFALL	16	14	14	9	8	6	4	4	7	11	14	18

4
The Aegean Coast

Turkey has over 500km (300 miles) of Aegean coastline, as well as a number of nearby islands. Much of the scenery here is typically **Mediterranean**: little inlets and coves, clear aquamarine sea and lovely, sandy beaches, overlooked by rocky slopes and olive groves. Like most of the Aegean, this is serious holiday territory. There aren't many utterly unspoilt spots – though a few still persist, if you're willing to venture off the beaten track.

Resorts such as **Kuşadası** and **Bodrum** are popular with the sun 'n fun set and, after Istanbul, nightlife in Turkey begins here.

Yet there's a lot more to this coast than sunburn and strobe lights. **Pergamon** and **Ephesus** are two of the finest ancient cities you'll see anywhere. Amid the extensive ruins and ancient streets, many buildings, temples and amphitheatres have remained virtually unchanged for 2000 years. Less well preserved, but even more evocative, is ancient **Troy,** where legendary Homeric ghosts haunt the fallen stones.

Another natural beauty is to be found inland at **Pamukkale**. Here spectacular terraced pools, formed by crystallized mineral salts, spill down the mountainside in suspended animation.

The main city in this region is **Izmir** (ancient Smyrna), which is the third largest city in Turkey. There are several good resorts located within easy reach of Izmir along the western peninsula which forms the Gulf of Izmir.

Don't Miss

*** **Ephesus:** considered by many to be the finest classical city still standing.
*** **Pamukkale:** the pools here, formed by mineral crystals, are Turkey's most spectacular natural blessing.
*** **Pergamon:** ancient city; its ruined temples rival those of the Acropolis in Athens.
** **Troy:** 3000 years ago this was the city which featured in Homer's epic *Iliad*.
* **Bodrum:** where the Turkish 'in' crowd come to play – along with the British crowds.

◀ *Opposite: The historic town of Bodrum is a favourite port of call on the Aegean Coast.*

The Rediscovery of Troy

For years it was believed that Homer's *Iliad* was just a myth. The German archaeologist Schliemann thought otherwise, however, and decided to follow certain geographical clues in the poem. In 1873 he located Troy. Schliemann started digging eagerly, reducing several layers of the ancient city to rubble in his enthusiasm. He discovered a hoard of priceless jewels, which he claimed were the treasure of King Priam. Later archaeologists, sifting through the debris, discovered that the treasure dated from the Bronze Age, about 2000BC, predating Priam by almost one thousand years.

NORTHERN AEGEAN COAST

Troy ★★

South of the Dardanelles the main road turns inland, and after a few miles you arrive at the ruins of Ancient Troy. As they stand, these are hardly the most impressive legacy from the ancient world, yet the rich legend they evoke easily makes up for this. Troy has atmosphere. We allegedly know what happened here over 3000 years ago – it's all there in Homer's *Iliad*. Today, you can supposedly see the gate through which the Trojans dragged the wooden horse and doomed themselves to defeat. There's even a model wooden horse outside the gate to make the point. However, Homer was writing centuries after the events he describes and archaeologists have proved that no fewer than nine consecutive cities have existed on this site, the first dating from the early Bronze Age over 5500 years ago. There is still even doubt about whether this was actually Troy.

Heinrich Schliemann had no such doubts. Hailed as a brilliant adventurer and expert archaeologist at the time, now seen more as a clumsy plunderer, he employed 150 workers and laboured for months, digging a railway line right through the site to help remove soil (thereby also removing much crucial evidence). However, he did find ruins aplenty and treasure which he shipped, along with the other finds, back to Germany. The gold disappeared in 1945 and was only rediscovered in Russia's Pushkin Museum after the Iron Curtain came down. Turkish efforts to retrieve it have so far met with a conspicuous lack of success. Meantime, excavations continue. (*See also* panel, page 65.)

▼ Below: Schliemann's trench, where the amateur German archaeologist conducted his dig at the site of ancient Troy in 1873.

Bozcaada ★★

You can catch a boat across to Bozcaada, the second of Turkey's Aegean islands from Çanakkale. The island is only about 12km (8 miles) in length, and has just one small town of cobbled streets overlooked by picturesque Ottoman balconies. Above the rooftops stands the imposing ruin of a 500-year-old **Venetian castle**.

The island's history goes back to Homeric times – this was where the Ancient Greek fleet hid, after they had left the wooden horse outside the walls of Troy. Bozcaada is hardly undiscovered, but it has yet to suffer the rigours and heavy demands of modern tourism. The island is justly renowned for its wines.

Back on the mainland, the road continues south to the coast, with some fine views out over the blue waters of the **Gulf of Edremit**, and follows the shoreline to the popular seaside resort of Ayvalık.

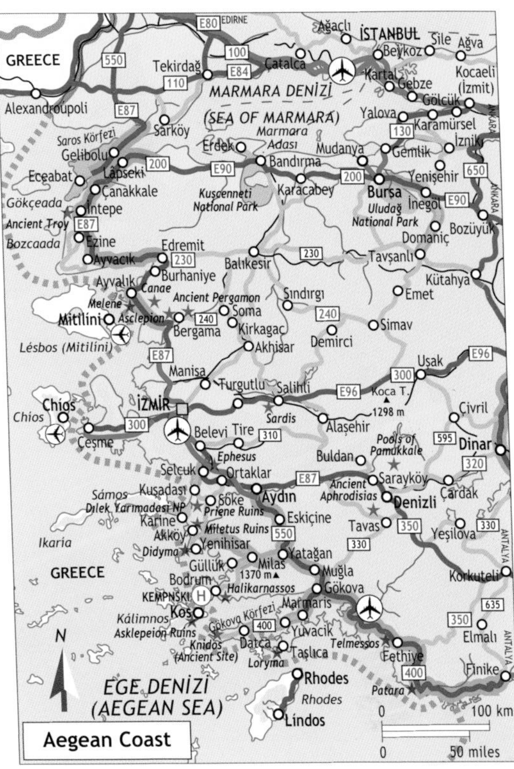

Ayvalık ★★

Ayvalık first began attracting the attention of tourists because of its exceptional beauty and comfortable amenities. And, despite the commercial efforts of the villa builders and the souvenir sellers, these remain largely intact and unspoilt. Ayvalık is tucked into a pleasant bay, with several good **beaches** nearby and half a dozen small **islands** around, all of which you can visit by boat. From the road heading to the south there are great views out over the sea towards the Greek island of **Lesbos**. The main beach resort is at **Sarımsaklı**, 8km (5 miles) south of town. There are a number of nice beaches along this stretch of coast, and some minor classical ruins off the road at **Melene** and **Canae**.

Climate

Summer in this region is **hot**, often unpleasantly so, maximum temperatures rising well above 30°C (86°F), especially in the south. The best time to visit is in the **spring** or **autumn**, when temperatures are around 23°C (73°F). At these times you can expect long sunny days, and the sea is warm enough for swimming. In winter temperatures drop and it's wet and windy.

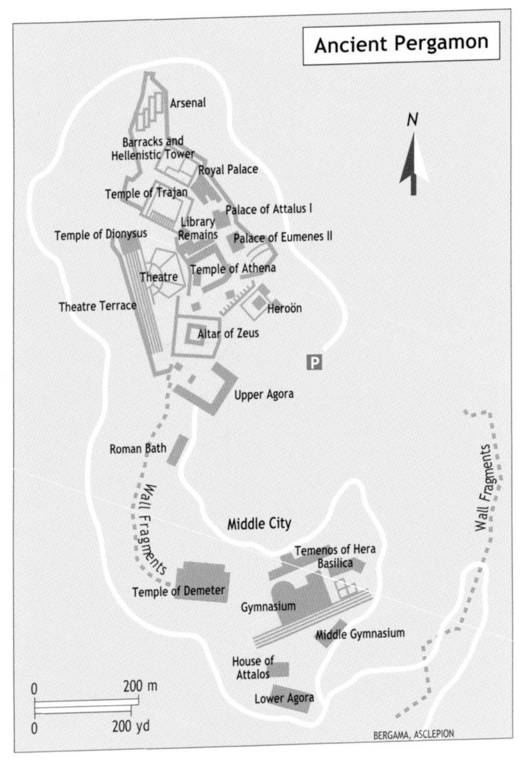

PERGAMON (BERGAMA)

About 36km (22 miles) south down the coastal road from Ayvalık, you turn off inland to reach Bergama. If you go by bus, it is wise to make sure that it goes all the way, or you will be dropped off 8km (5 miles) from the archaeological site on the outskirts of town. On the hillside above modern Bergama stands ancient **Pergamon**, whose ruins rate among the finest in the entire Mediterranean region and their situation, high on the bluff overlooking the surrounding plain, is as striking as any found on the Aegean seaboard.

The original settlement was founded by the Greeks as early as the 8th century BC, but it was to be another four centuries before the city rose to prominence, as a result of stolen treasure. After the death of **Alexander the Great,** his general, **Lysimachus**, left Alexander's entire fortune in the charge of his trusted eunuch **Philetarus**, while he himself set off to campaign in Syria. When Lysimachus was killed, Philetarus refused to surrender the 10,000 gold talents he was guarding, and instead started the building project which established Pergamon's greatness.

During the ensuing centuries Pergamon extended its territory, until by 190BC it ruled an empire covering almost half of Asia Minor. The city developed into one of the main cultural centres of the Ancient World, with superb temples and public buildings.

The **library** at Pergamon became second only to the great library at Alexandria. Indeed, the rivalry between these two bastions of classical learning soon became so fierce that the Alexandrians even blocked the export of papyrus from Egypt to Pergamon. Nowadays nothing but a few stones are left of this great library.

The Acropolis ★★

Fortunately, many of Pergamon's fine buildings have survived the ravages of time and conquest, among them the slender marble columns of **Trajan's Temple**. But the best reminder of the sheer size and splendour of ancient Pergamon is its superb **theatre**, whose terraced rows of seats are carved in a great arc into the hillside overlooking the valley below. In its heyday this theatre seated over 10,000 spectators and even today it retains splendid acoustics – try it out yourself. The river below was dammed then, creating an artificial lake on which naval galleons, manned by hundreds of gladiators and galley slaves, would engage in bloody battles.

The greatest building of all at Pergamon was the **Temple of Zeus**, which is mentioned in the Bible's Book of Revelations as 'the place where Satan has his altar'. All that remains today is the altar's foundation, which nonetheless makes an impressive sight.

The Face That Launched a Thousand Ships

According to Homer's *Iliad*, Paris abducted Helen, the beautiful wife of King Menelaus of Sparta, and carried her back to Troy. Menelaus summoned his Greek allies Odysseus, Achilles and Agamemnon and with a large army they sailed across the Aegean in 1000 ships to besiege Troy. The siege dragged on unsuccessfully for years (and dozens of verses of Homer), until the Greeks pretended to give up and sailed away, leaving behind a large wooden horse. The Trojans dragged the curious effigy into the city. That night, soldiers concealed inside its belly slipped out and opened the city gates to admit the Greek army, which had returned under the cover of darkness.

◀◀ Opposite: Pergamon's Trajan's Temple retains its delicate marble columns.
◀ Left: The ancient amphitheatre of Pergamon sits high above the modern town of Bergama.

A New Form of Paper

In the Ancient World, books were written on **papyrus** made of the bullrushes from the Nile Delta. When the jealous Egyptians boycotted the supply of papyrus to the rival library of Pergamon, librarians here were unable to produce any further scrolls. To overcome this hindrance, a new way of treating animal hides was invented. The new material became known as *pergamene*, which is the origin of our word parchment.

The **Acropolis** lies at the end of the curving road which ascends for 5km (3 miles) from the modern town. All the main monuments are within easy walking distance of one another, but if you wish you can also explore the remains of the **Gymnasium** (school) and the **Lower Agora** (market place) further down the hill towards Bergama. These tend to be less crowded and can easily be reached in 10 minutes. Open 08:30–17:30 daily; to 19:00 in summer.

The Archaeological Museum ★★

The modern town of Bergama is also worth a stop, with an excellent market, the **Red Basilica**, a 2nd–3rd-century church converted into a Byzantine basilica and an interesting Archaeological Museum on the main street. It contains a varied collection of more recent local finds. These may not match the pillaged masterpieces, now on show in Berlin's Pergamon Museum, but there is some interesting portraiture, including a bust of Socrates and a statue of the Emperor Hadrian. The little outside café here is a delight, with tables created from ancient pillar segments. Open 08:30–12:00 and 13:00–17:00, closed Mondays.

▼ Below: A superb Roman statue depicting the Emperor Hadrian stands on display in Bergama's Archaeological Museum.

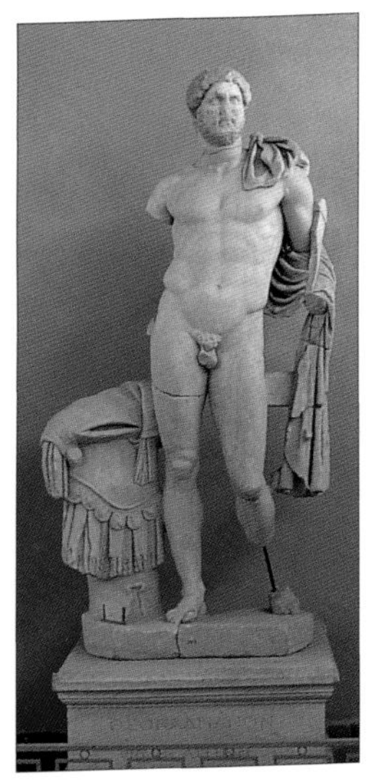

The Asceplion ★

On the other side of the valley from the main Acropolis, about 20 minutes' walk uphill from the Archaeological Museum, are the ruins of the Asclepion (*see also* panel, page 68). This temple dates from the 4th century BC and is dedicated to Asclepius, the son of Apollo, who was the Greek god of Healing. (His emblem, a snake curled about a winged staff, still adorns many a modern chemist shop.) The Asclepion at Pergamon was one of the great healing centres of the Ancient World. Medical science, then in its infancy, was a blend of quackery and primitive cures. Many rituals were conducted on this site, one of which involved walking through a tunnel (still in existence), while a physician whispered a cure in the patient's ear. Yet the techniques developed here were to produce the first great physician in Western history: Galen.

IZMIR

Izmir is Turkey's main Mediterranean port, the Turkish headquarters of **NATO**, and the third largest city in the country, after Istanbul and Ankara. The heart of Izmir is Konak, with its Clock Tower. The old Asansör district was the Jewish quarter, and has now been beautifully restored in period style. The Asansör (elevator) itself was built in the 19th century and the 50m (164ft) stairway provides access from the lower pedestrian precinct. A community of Greeks lived in Izmir until 1922 and the most famous one was Aristotle Onassis. The Onassis family were wealthy tobacco merchants and Ari himself was born in Smyrna, his first language being Turkish. He was about 20 when the family joined the stream of refugees fleeing the city before Atatürk's advancing armies. Most of the city was burned and over 30,000 people perished in the fire.

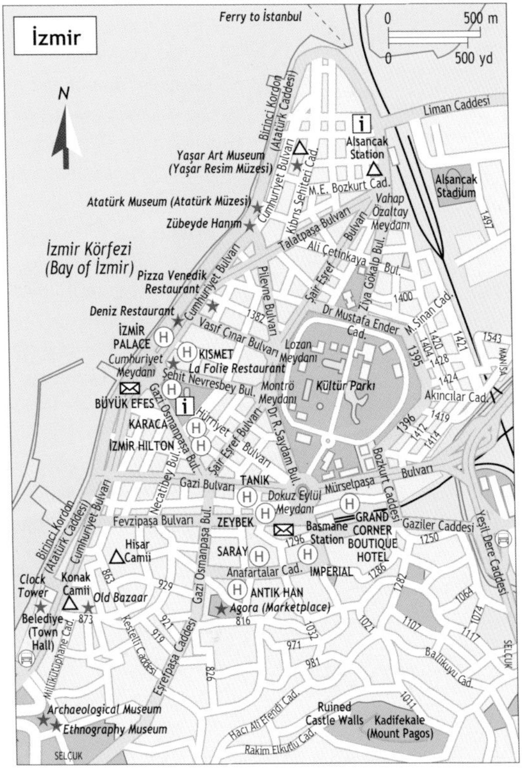

After being somewhat drab for several years, Izmir has regained some if its *beau monde* atmosphere. As you stroll around the streets of Alsancak or the Kordon Promenade, you could be anywhere in Europe with cafés and restaurants to match.

Izmir has plans to become a high-profile international technology capital, with preparations well under way for a biomedical technology park and a bid to host Expo 2020.

The Discovery of Pergamon

Pergamon was rediscovered by accident in 1871. **Karl Humann**, the German engineer building the Istanbul-Izmir railway, ran out of stone and sent his labourers into the nearby hills. They returned with exquisitely carved blocks of marble. He set off to search for the source and found the ruins of one of the ancient world's greatest cities.

▲ *Above: Izmir's modern town hall.*
▶ *Opposite: Ilıca Beach in Çeşme.*

The Archaeological and Ethnographic Museums ★

These museums lie five minutes' walk south of **Karşıyaka ferry terminal**. Both open 08:30–12:00 and 13:00–17:00, closed Mondays.

The **Archaeological Museum**, near Konak Square, has a superb collection of local antiquities, along with a Roman mosaic and fine classical statues, such as a 2nd-century impression of Poseidon and Demeter, a statue of a Roman Priest and a bronze Runner.

The **Ethnography Museum** across the road is in a former late-Ottoman hospital. Reconstructed dwellings and photos depict Izmir before 1922. There's also a reconstructed **Ottoman chemist's shop**.

The Bazaar ★★

Some 400m (438yd) north of the museums lies the bazaar quarter, the largest in the country outside Istanbul. Here you'll find the best **jewellers**. This, and the area just to the south, are best for **leatherwear** (jackets and shoes). In the back alleys you'll find vendors hawking everything from school exercise books and obscure fuses to live ducks. East of the Bazaar lies the ancient **Agora** (open 08:30–12:00, 13:00–17:00 daily), built by Alexander the Great in the 4th century BC; what remains today dates from the rebuilding by Marcus Aurelius after an earthquake in AD178. Several of the more complete Roman shops near the entrance to the Agora are being restored and reopened for business.

Kadifekale (Mount Pagos) ★

High above the city stands Kadifekale (which in Turkish means 'velvet castle'). At night, this ruined 500-year-old castle is floodlit, making it an impressive landmark. But the best time to visit this site is during the late afternoon, when you can watch the beautiful sunset over the city and hear the muezzins calling from the minarets. Regular dolmuşes run from Konak by the waterfront.

Greatest Physician of the Ancient World

Galen was born about 129BC, and underwent his medical apprenticeship at the Asclepion in Pergamon. He rapidly achieved such renown for his healing skills that he was invited to Rome to treat the emperor. Galen's treatises on medical practice were so profound that they became the standard works and were to remain so until the end of the Middle Ages, 1500 years after they had been written. He was the first to discover that arteries carry blood, not air as had been thought until then. He also dissected pigs and Barbary apes to learn about anatomy.

ÇEŞME PENINSULA

If you wish to get away from the heat and bustle of Izmir, you can always head for Çeşme, situated at the end of the peninsula that forms the Gulf of Izmir. Along here are many pleasant beaches and attractive small resorts, such as Ilıca, which has thermal hot springs and several excellent spa hotels.

SARDIS

Inland, on the road leading to **Salihli**, are the ruins of ancient Sardis (open 08:00–12:00 and 13:00–17:00 daily). This was the city once ruled by the legendary **Croesus** (*see* panel, page 70), the richest king in the ancient world, whose name has now become synonymous with opulence. In ancient times, minute particles of alluvial gold washed down the streams and rivers from the mountains in this region, and were collected in sheepskins by the **Lydians**. It is thought that this practice gave rise to the legend of the **Golden Fleece**, which was sought by **Jason and the Argonauts**.

The Muezzin's Call

One of the most atmospheric characteristics of the Muslim Middle East is the muezzin's call. Five times a day you will hear the muezzin's strident ululating call ringing out over the rooftops from a nearby minaret, summoning the faithful to prayer. The first sounds at daybreak, and is particularly evocative in the dreamlike transition from dark to light. Like it or not, this is one of the few experiences a visitor to the Middle East is unlikely to forget.

EPHESUS (EFES)

The site of ancient Ephesus lies approximately 16km (10 miles) northeast of the popular coastal resort of **Kuşadası**. It is the view of many experts that Ephesus is one of the best preserved of all the ancient classical cities, outshining even Pompeii for grandeur.

Around the end of the 1st century BC, Ephesus had a population of almost a third of a million and was one of the main ports along the Aegean coast. Then the sea began to recede across the flat plain of the **Menderes River** (this process has continued so that the

What's in a Name?

Nowadays, a person of great wealth is often said to be 'as rich as Croesus'. Croesus was once the fabulously wealthy King of Sardis. Just south of Izmir is the winding river Menderes, which in classical times used to be called the Meander, from which our term 'meander' derives. King Tantalus of Magnesia was doomed to *Hades* (hell) for murdering his sons. Here a delicious banquet was laid out before him, but each time he leaned forward to quench his thirst and still his hunger, it receded just beyond his reach, hence the word 'tantalize'.

ruins of Ephesus are now several kilometres away from the sea). The silting up of the port spelt the city's ruin, and it was ultimately abandoned. However, for us this disaster was a blessing. No invading army wished to waste its time destroying a deserted city, thereby preserving its ruins for generations to come. The finest of all is undoubtedly the **Library of Celsus**, with its delicately pillared façade and intricately carved interior. The nearby **Arcadian Way**, which is lined with columns, once led down to the sea. Also not to be missed are the **Lower Agora** and the 25,000-seat **theatre** carved into the mountain, which are at the inland end of the Arcadian Way. On a slightly less elevated plane but equally interesting is the nearby row of ancient Public Lavatories, and the inevitable Bordello.

Meryemana (Virgin Mary's House) ★

St Paul as well as the evangelists St Luke and St John spent time here and **St Luke** is thought to have paid several visits to Ephesus. Outside the back gate is the building which is thought to be St Luke's tomb. Even more intriguing is the legend that **St John** brought the aging **Virgin Mary** to Ephesus. Some 5km (3 miles) east of the ancient ruins lies the **Meryemana** (*see* panel, page 72), the house where Mary is said to have spent the last years of her life. In 1967, Pope Paul VI visited the site and gave it the official approval of the Catholic Church by declaring it authentic.

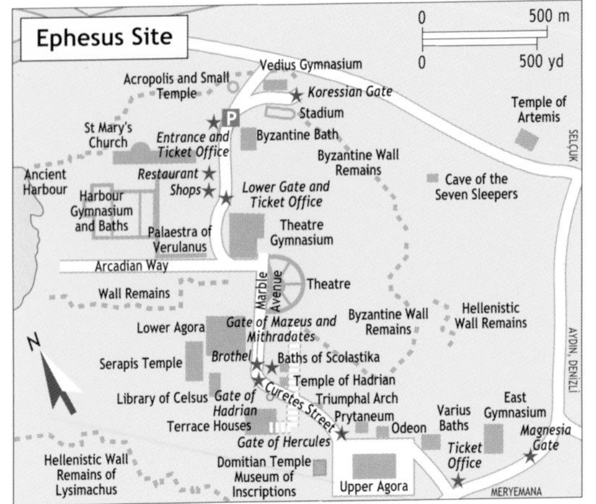

Selçuk ★★

Nearby Selçuk has a fine ancient citadel, which towers above the modern town. You can visit the **Basilica of St John**, a 6th-century Byzantine Church

◀ Left: The façade of the Library of Celsus at Ephesus, one of the most evocative ancient sites in the world.

built on the site of **St John's tomb**, the location of which is indicated by a marble slab. This region was also the site of one of the Seven Wonders of the Ancient World. The magnificent **Temple of Artemis** (Diana) attracted pilgrims from all over the Near East. The site is today but a field of scrub halfway between Selçuk and Ephesus.

In the centre of town is the **Archaeological Museum**, containing some of the racier relics in Turkey. The likeness of **Priapus** (god of phallic fun) has long been a favourite with visitors. Open daily 08:30–18:30.

Another attraction is the serious camel wrestling that takes place in Selçuk during January and February.

The Seven Sleepers' Cave

A few hundred metres east of the Ephesus site is a cave. It's said that during Roman times, seven early Christians hid here to avoid persecution and fell asleep while they waited. When they awoke, they returned to Ephesus, but noticed that everyone was wearing strange clothes. When they enquired about this latest fashion, they discovered that they had been asleep for 200 years. In the meantime, Christianity had become the state religion and they were safe.

SOUTHERN AEGEAN COAST

Kuşadası ★

Not long ago, Kuşadası was a sleepy fishing village, guarded by the tumbledown ruin of a **Genoese castle.** Now it is the liveliest **resort** on the Turkish Aegean coast and large **cruise liners** put in during the summer season. The coast around Kuşadası is blessed with a number of superb **beaches**, many of which are now overlooked by large modern resort hotel complexes. The town itself is within easy reach of Ephesus and Selçuk, as well as many other interesting sights further inland. It even has a few historic sites of its own. The old Genoese castle on the island of **Güvercin** has now been restored, and at night its floodlit battlements are

Coin Sellers

These are particularly prevalent at the approaches to Ephesus. A character will sidle up and show you surprisingly authentic-looking ancient coins. Few of these specimens *are* authentic, but you will face a long **jail sentence** if you try to take them out of the country. Most are clever fakes, stamped out from forgers' dies – but they are priced as if they were genuine. Either way, it's not worth it.

reflected in the waters of the bay beyond the coloured lights of the cruise liners. Close by the harbour the ancient **Kervansaray** (a former hostelry for the caravans of travelling merchants) has now been tastefully transformed into a luxury hotel.

Just south of Kuşadası are some of the best and most popular **beaches** on the Aegean coast. If you have time, visit the Dilek Peninsula National Park. The last of Turkey's wild horses roam here, as well as some other dwindling animal and bird species.

A Mysterious Vision

In the early 19th century a German nun, **Catherine Emmerich** had a detailed vision of the house where the Virgin Mary had lived in her old age. Almost a century later some Lazarist monks came to Selçuk to investigate the legend that had the Virgin Mary spending the last years of her life here. To their amazement they discovered a house that precisely matched the one Catherine had described. This house is today known as the Meryemana.

Priene ★

This site lies approximately 24km (15 miles) south of Kuşadası and is the most picturesque classical site in the region, even if it is of little historical significance. Priene stands on wooded hills above the sweeping valley of the scenic Menderes River.

Miletus (Milet) ★

Another nearby ancient city is Miletus, birthplace of the first Ancient Greek philosopher, Thales. This was once one of the greatest trading centres in the Mediterranean, with distant colonies in Egypt and the south of France. Like many Mediterranean harbours, it became inaccessible to merchant ships when it silted up.

Didyma (Didim) ★★

Just to the south of Kuşadası lie the ruins of Didyma with its famous pillared temple, built by Alexander the Great. Further south from here is one of the finest beaches in the region – **Altınkum Plaj** (Beach of the Golden Sands), a destination killed by its own success as Brits and other northern Europeans covered its natural beauty in vast suburban estates of identikit villas.

The Pools of Pamukkale ★★★

▲ *Above: The unique pools of Pamukkale, known for their curative properties since ancient times.*

◀ *Opposite: Sea, sun and sand at Altınkum beach.*

Some 150km (95 miles) east of Kuşadası lies the sight which adorns many travel posters: pools of blinding white crystal spilling down the mountainside. They receive their water from the warm springs nearby, whose minerals have gradually become encrusted along the limestone slopes, forming these spectacular, **terraced pools**. Since the enthusiastic hordes of tourists have been banned from climbing on this spectacular 'cotton castle', it is gradually regaining its pristine appearance (you may paddle in one carefully restricted area, without shoes). The whole area was, and still is, a spa. It is possible to swim in the Antique Pool behind the falls. The cascade shares the plateau with ancient **Hierapolis**, a trendy Graeco-Roman spa town, with an imposingly large necropolis, which would suggest that the cure was not always effective. Further back along the plateau, the village of **Karahayıt** also has travertine falls, though far smaller and multicoloured, and has been overrun by hotels, most of them spas.

APHRODISIAS

About 150km (95 miles) inland from Ephesus are the ruins of ancient Aphrodisias. In Roman times, this was one of the main centres for the worship of Aphrodite, goddess of love and fertility, to whom the city was dedicated. Aphrodisias yielded some of the richest treasures uncovered in excavations. The area comprises the **Temple of Aphrodite**, monuments, a theatre and baths. There is also a spectacular **stadium** where athletics rivalling the Olympic Games were staged. The museum houses superb marble works. Open daily Apr–Oct 08:00–19:00, Nov–Mar

Oriental Splendour

A Swedish marketing consultant working in Izmir remembers that his grandparents had planned a grand honeymoon to take in all the major capitals of Europe, and these included Paris, Vienna and Smyrna (Izmir, *see* page 67). Before World War I, Izmir was one of the most cosmopolitan capitals in Europe, deservedly famous for its culture, class and ethnic diversity.

▲ *Above: Aphrodisias's stadium was once a venue for glorious athletic games.*

08:00–17:00. Aphrodisias became the seat of one of the greatest schools of sculpting during the classical era. It is less crowded here than at Pergamon and Ephesus, and some parts are better preserved.

BODRUM

Approximately 150km (95 miles) south of Kuşadası lies the chic harbour resort of Bodrum, whose name means 'dungeon'. In former times this was a place of exile for courtiers and ministers who had fallen foul of the Sultan in Istanbul.

Despite extensive development the town retains its charm, and whitewashed houses cluster on the hillside above an ancient harbour with its **Crusader castle**. The modern town stands on the site of the ancient Greek city of **Halicarnassos**, which was established as long ago as the 11th century BC. Several centuries later the Greek historian **Herodotus,** whose chronicles earned him the title 'Father of History', was born here.

From the waterfront at Bodrum you can take **boat trips** to the nearby islands and along the spectacularly beautiful coastline.

The Ertegün Brothers

Ahmet and Nesuhi Ertegün grew up in Bodrum. When their father became Turkish ambassador to the United States in the 1930s, the family moved to America. Here the brothers became so enraptured with American jazz that they set up their own record company: **Atlantic**. Within 30 years Atlantic had become one of the most influential labels in the business, featuring such stars as **Johnny Coltrane** and the **Modern Jazz Quartet**. Nesuhi died in 1989 and Ahmet in 2006.

Castle of St Peter ★★★

This castle was started by the Crusaders in the early 15th century and completed in 1522. No sooner was it complete, than the Crusaders abandoned it, because Süleyman the Magnificent had captured their stronghold at Rhodes, so this outpost was no longer considered worth defending.

The structure remains largely intact. It also houses the **Museum of Underwater Archaeology**, a superb collection of underwater treasures from the many vessels which sank off the Aegean and Mediterranean coasts. Each hall in the castle is devoted to a different era –

from the Mycenaean age onward including the tomb treasure of a 4th-century BC princess, possibly the wife or sister of King Mausolus. Open 08:30–12:00 and 13:00–17:00 Tuesday–Sunday (different sections open on different days and cannot always be guaranteed to open even when they say they will, so check locally).

The Mausoleum ★★

During the 4th century BC, Bodrum was ruled by **King Mausolus**, who built himself a tomb of such splendid magnificence that it became one of the Seven Wonders of the Ancient World. It was known as the **Mausoleum**, and is the origin of the word we use to describe a grandiose tomb. Nearly 2000 years later, the Crusaders used stones from the ruined Mausoleum to build the castle which still guards the harbour. Little remains of the Mausoleum but its foundations. Despite this, the site is worth a visit, if only for the small exhibition which fills in the historical detail and contains models of the original treasures removed by archaeologists. It lies a short walk inland from the harbour on **Turgutreis Caddesi**. Open daily Apr–Oct 08:00–19:00, Nov–Mar 08:00–17:00. Closed Mondays.

APHRODITE

Aphrodite was the ancient Greek name for **Venus**, whose name is much more recognizable to us as the goddess of love. The old Greek name is the origin of our word 'aphrodisiac', which means 'love potion'.

MUĞLA

Some 100km (65 miles) across the mountains lies Muğla, with some fine old wooden houses in its winding back streets. But the best thing to see here is the extensive **market** held every Thursday, one of the finest of its kind in provincial Turkey. Old women in traditional peasant dress come down from the mountains to sell peppers. Perfume and spice sellers set up their stalls here, and local craftware is for sale at excellent prices.

▼ *Below: This romantic Crusaders' Castle lies at the entrance to Bodrum harbour.*

THE AEGEAN COAST AT A GLANCE

Best Times to Visit

The Aegean coast of Turkey can become very hot indeed in summer, with temperatures regularly around 30°C (86°F). In winter it cools down somewhat, but is often rainy. By far the best times to visit this region are **spring** (March to the end of May), or **autumn** (September to mid-November).

Getting There

There are regular international flights to Istanbul and Izmir as well as a few scheduled services to Pamukkale and Bodrum-Muğla, which really comes into its own catering to chartered flights in summer. You could also fly in to Dalaman for some southern areas. In winter there are very few options and you may well have to change planes. There are buses from Adnan Menderes Airport into Izmir, but most find it easier to arrange a transfer with their hotel or hire a car. The train to Selçuk passes through the airport but services are infrequent. Contact Turkish Airlines 24-hour central reservations, tel: 212 444 0849, www.thy.com.tr

Getting Around

All the airports have car hire facilities, but you may also hire a vehicle at any main resort. All the Aegean region and its sights are well connected by comfortable and regular bus services and dolmuşes. The hub is Izmir's bus terminal (Otogar) on the southwestern side of the city. Even for Ephesus, don't rule out a guided tour, as public transport will drop you a few kilometres from the main entrance. Another reason for an organized tour is that you can also take in the Virgin Mary's House, which is remote and not accessible by any public transport. If you are going out of the region, to Istanbul, say, you must make a reservation at one of the bus companies' city-centre offices and their free shuttle service will deliver you to the terminal. If you have time to spare and want a trip back in time, go by rail from Izmir to Denizli. Trains leave from the main train station in Basmane. They are inexpensive but take much longer than the bus. Pammukale and Aphrodisias, however, are further from Izmir. Unless you have a rental car, try to see these places with a tour group. Setur is one of the more imaginative ones.

Where to Stay

Ayvacık

Mid-range

Berceste Hotel, Sivrice Feneri MV, Bektas Köyü, 17860, Ayvacık, tel: 286 723 4616, www.bercestehotel.com Set on a hillside overlooking the tiny village of Sivrice, near Assos, with fabulous sea views and a pebble beach only 400m away (downhill), this simple stone-built guesthouse is a delightful hideaway from the usual run of Turkish hotels and an ideal place from which to explore the north Aegean.

Pamukkale

Budget

Venüs Hotel, Pamuk Mh. Hasan Tahsin Cad. 16, Pamukkale, tel: 258 272 2152, www.venushotel.net Small friendly, family-run pension in Pamukkale village with a garden and pool.

Kuşadası

Mid-range

Vista Hill Hotel, Yavansu Mah. Suleyman Demirel Blv. No 154, tel: 256 622 0505, www.booking.com Large all-inclusive seafront resort hotel with all the trimmings – an excellent example of the species with a great pool, food and service.

Villa Konak, Yıldırım Caddesi 55, tel: 256 614 6318, www.villakonakhotel.com Attractive old town mansion with restaurant, garden and pool. Rooms set around small courtyards.

Bodrum

Luxury

Antique Theatre Hotel, Kıbrıs Şehitler Caddesi 243, Bodrum, tel: 252 316 6053/4, www.antiquetheatrehotel.com A real gem in a high-rise jungle.

Kempinski Hotel Barbaros Bay, Kizilagac Köyü Gerenkuyu Mevkii, 48400 Bodrum, tel: 252 311 0303, www.kempinski-bodrum.com This is a luxurious hotel with a lavish Six Senses spa, several superb restaurants and a private beach, located about 15 minutes' drive from the town centre.

Çeşme

LUXURY

Sheraton Çeşme, Sifme Caddesi 35, Ilıca, tel: 232 723 1240, www.sheratoncesme.com Large, sumptuous five-star resort, just out of town, with all the trimmings – from a private beach to a magnificent spa.

MID-RANGE

Vintage Hotel Alaçati, Yenimecidiye Mahallesi, 3046 Sokak No 2 , Alaçati, tel: 0203 027 8675, www.vintagealacati.com Tiny town centre boutique hotel within walking distance of the beach. Eight beautifully designed rooms, restaurant and garden.

Izmir

MID-RANGE

Grand Corner Boutique Hotel, Anafartalar Caddesi No 783, Basmane, tel: 232 484 4141, www.grandcornerhotel.com New town centre hotel with flamboyant décor, restaurant, hamam and helpful, smiling staff.

Crown Plaza Izmir, Inciraltı Caddesi 67, 35340 Balçova, Izmir, tel: 232 292 1300, www.cpizmir.com One of several new five-star hotels to open in the city, this round tower is one of the most luxurious, with three restaurants, three bars, a pool, spa and regular shuttle into the city centre.

Selçuk (for Ephesus)

Hotel Kale Han, Atatürk Caddesi 49, Selçuk, tel: 232 892 6154, www.kalehan.com Restored in authentic style.

Nisanyan Evleri Hotel, Sirince, tel: 232 898 3208, www.nisanyan.com Magical country hideaway, 8km from Ephesus, offering accommodation in a range of restored village houses, with gourmet dining from a choice of local restaurants.

WHERE TO EAT

Asansör Ceneviz Meyhanesi, Mithatpaşa Cad. Dario Moreno Sok, Izmir, tel: 232 255 5420. The view is unsurpassed from this popular restaurant at the top of the Asansör, the elevator that joins the upper and lower parts of Izmir – oh, and the food is good too!

Bulbul Restaurant, Alacamescit Mh. Kahramanlar Cad. No 84/A, Kuşadası, tel: 256 613 0095. A bit off the beaten track, but this is a real Turkish favourite with authentic and very good local cuisine.

Mimoza, Yalı Mevkii 44/1, Gümüşlük, tel: 252 394 3139, www.mimozagumusluk.com Not a cheap option, but probably the finest seafood restaurant on the whole Bodrum peninsula (no mean feat), with a fabulous waterfront setting perfect for watching the sunset.

Sünger Pizza, Neyzen Tevfik Caddesi 216, Bodrum, tel: 252 316 0854, www.sungerpizza.com This eatery is open all day every day; excellent pizzas and good meat and seafood; popular and affordable.

USEFUL CONTACTS

Tourist Information Offices:

Izmir, Gaziosmanpaşa Bulvarı No 1/1 Efes Oteli Altı, tel: 232 445 7390.

Adnan Menderes Airport, tel: 232 274 2214.

Kuşadası, Iskele Meydanı, tel: 256 614 1103.

Bodrum, Barış Meydanı, tel: 252 316 1091,

Çeşme, Iskele Meydanı, tel: 232 712 6653,

Turkish Airlines: 24-hour central reservations tel: 212 444 0849, www.thy.com.tr

Tour Companies and Travel Agents:

Bodrum Tour, Carsi MH. Uckuyular Street No 7/B, Bodrum, tel: 252 313 3009, www.bodrumtour.com

Kuşadası Tours, Turkmen Mh. Candan Tarhan Bul. Seharazat Ap. No 1-2, Kusadası Aydin 09400, www.kusadasitours.com

Bodtur, Cumhuriyet Bul. 242/1, D 3, Alsancak, Izmir, tel: 232 421 8002, www.bodtur.com

IZMIR	J	F	M	A	M	J	J	A	S	O	N	D
AVERAGE TEMP. °F	55	57	63	70	79	87	92	92	85	76	67	58
AVERAGE TEMP. °C	13	14	17	21	26	31	33	33	29	24	19	14
RAINFALL in	4	3	3	2	1	6	2	2	8	2	3	5
RAINFALL mm	112	84	76	43	33	15	50	50	206	53	84	122
DAYS OF RAINFALL	10	8	7	5	4	2	1	1	2	4	6	10

5 The Mediterranean Coast

The western stretch of Turkey's Mediterranean region contains the **Turquoise Coast**, an area of exceptional maritime beauty with numerous picturesque beaches and inlets. Best known of these is **Ölüdeniz**, with its spectacular lagoon. This coastline is very popular with yachting enthusiasts, as many of the more remote beaches and coves can only be reached from the sea. In this region you will find lively nightlife as well as lazy, sun-filled days on some of Turkey's finest beaches.

The main resorts (and yachting centres) on this western section of the coast are **Marmaris**, **Fethiye** and **Dalyan**. Further east are the charming little towns of **Kalkan** and **Kaş**, with the tiny Greek island of **Meis** (Kastellorizo) just offshore. East of here is the island of **Kekova**, where the remains of a Byzantine city are visible beneath the water.

Between Fethiye and **Antalya** are dozens of classical sites. Most of these date from the 1st millennium BC, when this stretch of coast was colonized by the Ancient Greeks. This was the home of the Lycians with their distinctive rock tombs visible everywhere. Some of the sites are in exceptionally remote and beautiful settings, and many have excellently preserved theatres and temples.

Belek is a golfing and nature paradise approximately 30km (19 miles) east of Antalya. There are a number of championship courses as well as splendid flora and fauna. At the eastern end of Turkey's Mediterranean coast you come to **Adana**. Here you are actually closer to Damascus than to Europe, and the region begins to take on a distinctly Eastern atmosphere.

Don't Miss

*** **Marmaris:** picturesque resort and yachting centre, makes an ideal base for exploring the coast.
*** **Tahtali and Phaselis:** Europe's longest cable-car run sweeps up above the ruins of ancient Phaselis.
*** **Ölüdeniz:** a scenically beautiful lagoon with good swimming beaches.
*** **Perge and Aspendos:** ancient cities with some of the Mediterranean's most spectacular ruins.
** **Belek:** visit the excellent golf courses in this nature preservation area.

◀ *Opposite: Sailing boats like this one are ideal for exploring the lovely coast.*

▲ *Above: Boats bask in the sun alongside the pleasant waterfront of Marmaris.*
▶ *Opposite: Marmaris has all the attractions of a developed resort, including plenty of shopping.*

MARMARIS

South of Muğla you come to the popular resort of Marmaris, situated at the end of a long inlet from the sea. Marmaris is a popular **yachting centre** and boasts the largest **marina** in Turkey. This is a very good yacht charter centre whether you want to sail yourself or hire a boat with a captain and crew. It is a wise sailor who makes his booking and signs a contract through a charter agent in his own country.

Marmaris is favoured with one of the finest natural harbours in the whole of the eastern Mediterranean. In the 16th century, Süleyman the Magnificent anchored the Turkish fleet here.

Modern Marmaris has a hectic nightlife, with many discos and some excellent restaurants along the front. You can also take day trips out to the nearby **Loryma Peninsula**, to the island beaches and also to Rhodes. Marmaris can easily be reached from Izmir, Bodrum or Dalaman airports (about 2 hours' drive from all).

The road leading from Muğla to Marmaris has really stunning views. Descending quite steeply to sea level after leaving the village of Gökova, it passes through Marmaris National Park, which has some of the lushest pine forests in Turkey.

TRIPS TO RHODES

During the summer, regular ferries run from Marmaris to the Greek island of Rhodes, only 50km (30 miles) across the Aegean, a pleasant day cruise. At the other end you are at leisure to explore the town of Rhodes, which has a lovely harbour and picturesque Old Town. This was the medieval stronghold of the Knights of St John. You can still visit the cobbled streets and quaint inns the knights frequented before setting off on their crusades to Jerusalem.

Datça ★★

To the south and west of Marmaris stretch the fat Bozburun Peninsula and long, skinny, mountainous Datça Peninsula, both lined by hotels and small resort villages for much of their length. Datça, once a tiny village, is now a thriving resort in its own right, with a lively nightlife scene. **Boat trips** to the more remote beaches further along the peninsula are available. The best of these is to the ancient site of **Knidos**, which lies at the very tip of the peninsula over 30km (18 miles) away. Some 3000 years ago Knidos was one of the richest cities in the eastern Mediterranean. Today it is a charming, secluded nook that hasn't forsaken its character for tourism.

The area is also known for health reasons, for it is off Datça that the Mediterranean Sea meets the Aegean. Due to the differing salt levels in the two seas and also the presence of underwater sea currents, the locals claim that the air is ultra rich in oxygen.

The Philosopher of Knidos

The ancient city of Knidos, at the tip of the Datça Peninsula, produced one of the greatest scholars of the early classical era. Eudoxus lived in the 4th century BC and was a pupil of Plato. This exceptional man was the first to explain the helio-centric movement of the planets, and also corrected the length of the solar year. Today his genius is largely forgotten however, as his ideas were plagiarized by the early Greek geometer Euclid, who is still credited with Eudoxus' discoveries.

Dalyan ★★

This is a quiet town on the waterway between the inland **Köyceğiz Lake** and the sea. Visit the ruins at nearby **Kaunos** via a short boat trip from Dalyan or Köyceğiz. From Marmaris, the trip takes a whole day. The journey takes you through shallow, reedy waterways from where you see excellent Lycian rock tombs over 1500 years old set high into the cliffs. Instead of burying their dead, Lycians believed they should continue in the next life alongside relatives and neighbours. Hence these tombs

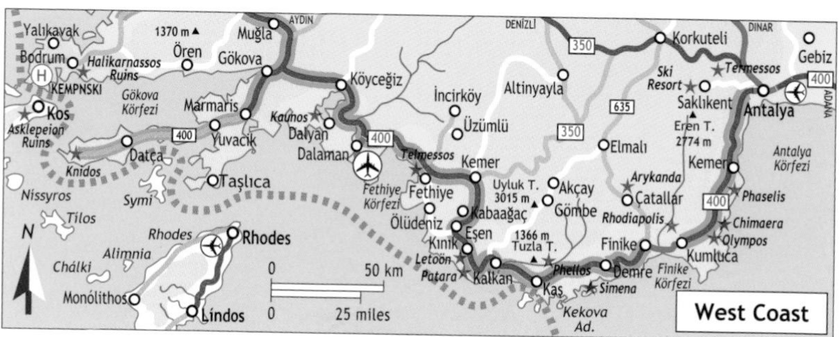

Climate

The **summers** are long and **very hot** along this stretch of coast, with temperatures often rising above 35°C (95°F). Winter however, brings storms and much cooler weather. The best time to visit is **spring**, which sees warm **sunny** days and flowers blooming on the hillsides. **Autumn** also has long warm **sunny** days.

are above ground. Kaunos was founded in the 9th century BC and was an important city in the Lycian Federation. Among the classical remains are a fine temple, a theatre, an acropolis and a massive Roman bath. The inhabitants were gradually killed off by malaria, endemic at the time.

From Dalyan, take a boat to **Turtle Beach** (*Istuzu*), the breeding ground of the rare **Loggerhead Turtles**. In **June** they come ashore at night to bury their eggs in the soft sand. Unscrupulous development of this area – which would have spelt certain death to the turtles – was halted by a vigorous campaign led by British naturalist David Bellamy. During nesting time, the beach is closed nightly from 22:00–08:00 to avoid disturbing the turtles.

Upriver from Köyceğiz are mud baths. A visit to these is more entertaining than medicinal.

TURQUOISE COAST

Fethiye ★★★

Bustling Fethiye has good shopping and restaurants, but the town is rather ordinary. Serious holiday-makers prefer to head 20km (12 miles) down the coast to Ölüdeniz.

Ölüdeniz ★★★

Some visitors lament the results of overenthusiastic tourism in Ölüdeniz ('dead sea' in Turkish), but drop

▼ *Below: A boat ride to the ancient ruins of Kaunos will take you past some fine examples of Lycian rock tombs.*

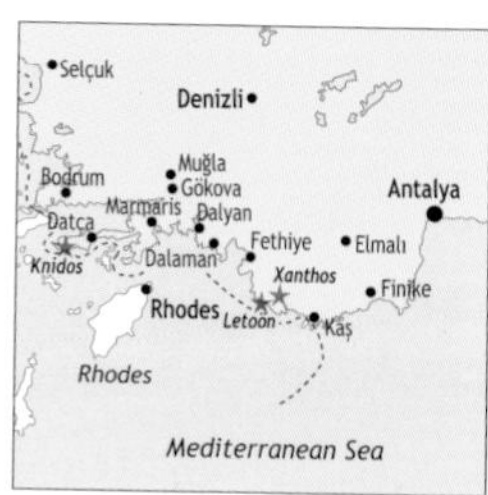

◀ *Left: One of Turkey's most photogenic spots, Ölüdeniz can be reached by a precipitous mountain road.*

down the steep mountain road to the stunningly beautiful lagoon and you've reached *the* major mass market family-friendly resort along the Lycian coast. The lagoon is protected by a national park but a vast array of clubs, hotels, aparthotels and pensions to suit a range of budgets crawl up the valley and spill over into neighbouring Hisaronu. If you are looking for a little more peace and quiet, try staying in the Greek ghost village of Kayaköy next door. As well as the usual tourist offerings, Ölüdeniz has great water sports and is a world-class centre for paragliding.

Xanthos ★

Xanthos lies approximately 40km (25 miles) to the east of Fethiye and is best accessed from the village of Kınık. Once the greatest city of Lycia, its former glory has now mostly been pillaged or suffered earthquake damage. An unrestored **obelisk** and **acropolis** lie among ruins from Lycian, Roman and Byzantine eras.

Letoön ★

Some 6km (3.5 miles) from Xanthos, Letoön houses the ruins of temples dedicated to **Leto, Apollo and Artemis**.

Patara ★

This was the principal harbour of ancient **Lycia** and is thought to be the birthplace of St Nicholas. Sand-embedded ruins are still being excavated and a stunning 22km (13-mile) stretch of sandy beach would be overrun with tourists if the water weren't so shallow.

Ancient Lycia

Lycia reached its apogee between 200 and 100BC. Landlocked by high mountains and reliant on sea trade, it was no wonder Lycia existed as an independent feudal fiefdom. Many killed themselves rather than submit to conquerors. Even when subdued by Alexander the Great, they retained their own language and culture. Their demise came not from enemies. When their principal harbour at Patara silted up, a vital lifeline to sea trade was gone. They left a legacy mostly of the strange rock and house tombs which dot the area.

▲ *Above: Kaş harbour is one of the jewels of the Mediterranean coast.*

Kaş and Kalkan ★★

Both Kaş and Kalkan were Greek villages before 1922 and still have pretty Byzantine churches, barely disguised by the present-day mosques. Both are now among Turkey's most sophisticated holiday resorts. Kalkan is more sedate, and offers some of the best cuisine on the coast. Kaş is known for its freewheeling nightlife and superb shopping. There are good examples of Lycian tombs and a **Hellenistic amphitheatre**.

Kaputaş

Between Kaş and Kalkan is a spectacular gorge that opens out onto a sandy beach at Kaputaş. There are 200 steps down to the unspoiled

Kekova and Simena ★★

Trips to Kekova run by boat from Kaş or by road (more difficult) from Ucağiz. Ruins include a **submerged Byzantine city**. At Kaleköy (Simena) are the ruins of a Crusader Castle with the world's smallest theatre, seating just 12.

Demre and Kale (Myra) ★★

Some 45km (28 miles) from Kaş, the village of Demre itself is uninteresting. But the Byzantine Church of St Nicholas is a delight. St Nicholas was based here as Bishop of Myra and died here in AD326. Ancient Myra, just out of town, has some excellent rock tombs and a fine little theatre.

Tahtali

While the hiking in the Beydağları Olympos National Park is superb, there is now an easier way to get up to the top: the 4350m **Tahtali Teleferik** (tel: 242 814 3047, open daily 10:00–18:00 winter, 09:00–19:00 summer; entry fee). From its base station near the Phaselis turn-off, it swings up from 736m (2425ft) above sea level to the summit of Mt Tahtali, at 2365m (7759 ft) the tallest mountain in the world that rises directly out of the sea, making it Europe's longest cable-car ride. The views are spectacular.

Olympos ★

Ancient history remains somewhat sketchy, but Olympos has been known as the eternal flame of the **Chimaera** since the 4th century BC. The flame (*Yanartaş* in Turkish), formed by continually self-igniting gas escaping from the hillside, still burns to this day. This is a leafy and cool retreat with a pebble beach, popular with backpackers.

Phaselis ★★

One of the prettiest if least known of the ancient cities along this coast, Phaselis is a delightful place, easily reached from Antalya, Olympos and the nearby resort of

Kemer. There are three small harbours on a wooded peninsula and just enough ruins for sightseeing between swims. Take a picnic and make a day of it. Open daily, Apr–Oct 09:00–19:00, Nov–Mar 08:30–17:00.

ANTALYA

Antalya, situated on a wide bay, is framed by high mountains to the west. The city looks down over a harbour, which has a **Roman lighthouse** on the hillside at its southeastern approach. The citizens of old Antalya were so renowned for their fighting qualities that they remained unconquered throughout most of the classical era. Even Alexander the Great decided against attacking them, and the Romans thought it best to adopt a diplomatic approach, welcoming them as 'allies'.

Glass Pyramid

One of Antalya's modern landmarks is the splendid glass pyramid, which houses the Sabanci Congress and Culture Centre. A variety of musical, artistic and film performances are staged here. It is the main venue for the opening and closing ceremonies of the Golden Orange Film Festival held every September in Antalya.

Kaleiçi ★

Around the harbour lies the **Old Quarter** with steep lanes, narrow winding streets and scattered Roman ruins. The main sight in Antalya is the famous **Yivli Minare** (Fluted Minaret), which is decorated with turquoise and dark blue tiles and dominates the slope above the harbour.

▼ *Below: The distinctive Yivli Minare rises above the houses of Antalya.*

Antalya Archaeological Museum ★★★

Don't miss this museum which houses one of Turkey's finest collections of antiquities dating from the Palaeolithic Age to Ottoman times. Some of the recent treasures repatriated to Turkey from abroad are also on display here. Allow at least an afternoon to appreciate this museum. It is open daily Apr–Oct 09:00–19:00, Nov–Mar 08:00–17:00. An entrance fee is payable.

AROUND ANTALYA

Perge and Aspendos ★★★

Along the coast to the south of Antalya are a growing number of good beach resorts. This region also has a number of fine classical ruins. The best of these is **Perge**, near Antalya airport, a successful trading city by 1300BC, which only died when its harbour silted up in the Byzantine era. There are some Greek remains, such as the huge red-brick gates, but most of the remains, such as the wonderfully preserved forum, stadium and theatre, are Roman. Open daily Apr–Oct 09:00–19:00; Nov–Mar 08:00–17:30.

Aspendos, about 30km (18 miles) further east, has one of the world's finest Roman theatres (*see* panel). Open daily Apr–Oct 09:00–19:00, Nov–Mar 08.00–17:00.

In nearby **Belkis** are several excellent shopping outlets for carpets, jewellery and fashion.

ASPENDOS

Between Fethiye and Antalya, there are over 40 important historical sites. The Roman theatre at Aspendos, some 47km (29 miles) east of Antalya, is one of the best preserved in the world. It was built by the architect Zeno at the end of the 2nd century AD. There is a perfectly preserved aqueduct, 850m (930yd) long. The theatre seats 20,000 and is the venue for the Aspendos Opera and Ballet Festival held every June and September (www.aspendosfestival.gov.tr).

Side ★

The name is a pre-Greek one meaning pomegranate, a symbol of fertility. Once the jewel tourist venue of this area, with lovely sandy beaches, Side has since deteriorated into an overdone tourist jungle. However, the **archaeological excavations** with their 2nd-century Roman theatre, **Temple of Apollo**, Agora and bath-house museum are worth a visit. The Temple Apollo on the seafront has spectacular sunset views.

▶ Opposite: Alanya's old castle perches high above the modern town.

▼ Below: Turkish carpets for sale in Side.

Belek ★

About 40km (25 miles) from the city of Antalya, the region around Belek is a golfer's paradise. The resort has an astonishing 17 golf courses, with no fewer than 11 of them at championship standard, all accessible and playable by the public. The area also offers some of the best hotels in the region and beautifully clean sandy beaches. You don't have to be a golfer to come here, as there is every sport under the sun.

CILICIA

Alanya ★

East from Antalya along Rt 400, after about 115km (72 miles) you reach Alanya. This town has three **beaches**, and endless out-of-town hotel developments.

In 44BC the besotted Roman general **Mark Antony** gave this entire region to his beloved Cleopatra, and in the 13th century it was captured by Sultan Alladin, who established his summer capital here. The citadel soars dizzyingly over the western edge of the Old City. The **Kızıl Kule** (Red Tower) dominates the eastern approach. This impressive 30m (100ft) construction was built in the early 13th century and remains largely intact. Just 10 minutes' walk north is a subterranean cavern aptly known as **Damlataş** (Cave of Dripping Stones), with some good stalactites. Open 10:00–18:00, 06:00–10:00 if taking the cure.

Ferries to Cyprus

From the west of Turkey's Mediterranean coast it is possible to catch ferries across to Northern Cyprus. This island is at present divided, and ferries from Turkey only put in on the northern side. It is possible to cross from the north to Greek Cyprus, but only if you agree to have your entry stamp/visa cancelled (i.e. you can't go back) – and even then it's a hassle. Regular ferries leave from **Taşuçu** 80km (50 miles) east of Anamur, and from **Mersin** 60km (37 miles) southwest of Adana.

Anamur ★★

Anamur lies 60km (37 miles) southeast of Alanya and is Turkey's southernmost point. West of the town lie the ruins of ancient Anemurium thought to have been founded by the Phoenicians. During the Roman era it became one of the most important cities in the eastern Mediterranean. Eight kilometres (5 miles) east of Anamur is **Mamure Kalesi**, one of the most romantic and best preserved Crusader castles in the entire Mediterranean. Open 09:30–17:30 daily.

Adana ★

This, the fourth largest city in Turkey, is mentioned in the Bible (King Solomon bought horses from here). **St Paul** came from Tarsus, 40km (25 miles) to the west.

The **Archaeological Museum** houses interesting exhibits, including some Hittite seals dating from the 15th century BC, but the city's prime attraction is the huge new **Sirkeci Merkez Camii** (Central Mosque), a gleaming heap of marble domes beside the river.

Best Times to Visit

The summers along this coastline can be unpleasantly hot, with temperatures regularly above 35°C (95°F). Winter means frequent storms, with temperatures dropping to 7°C (45°F). Best times to visit are **spring** or **autumn**, when there are usually warm, **sunny** days.

Getting There

There are regular international flights to Adana, Alanya, Antalya and Dalaman. Antalya's Bayındır International Airport rivals any in Europe.

Getting Around

No trains on this mountainous coast. Air-conditioned coaches ply the main roads between resorts and there are armies of dolmuş for local transport. All local tour operators offer airport transfers and a wide assortment of day trips. All the main car hire companies have offices at the airports.

Where to Stay

Marmaris

Luxury

Grand Pasa Hotel, Durmazlar Caddesi 15, 48700 Marmaris, tel: 252 417 7227, www.grandpasahotel.com A seamlessly luxurious five-star resort 3.5km from the town centre; 350m from the beach.

Sabrinas Haus, Bozburun, Adatepe, Marmaris, tel: 252 456 2045/2470, www.sabrinashaus.com Also known as the Elixir Art Hotel (www.elixirarthotel.com), this chic little seafront boutiqie hotel is a perfect fantasy hideaway.

Budget

Terrasses de Selimiye Butik Hotel, Selimiye Koyu Marmaris Merkez, tel: 252 446 4367, www.selimiyepension.com Beautiful boutique hotel (11 rooms) with terraces cascading down to a private beach in a small village near Marmaris. Restaurant, pool.

Fethiye/Ölüdeniz

Luxury

Hotel Montana Pine Resort, Ovacık Mahallesi, Ölüdeniz Beldesi, tel: 252 616 7108, www.montanapine.com Comfortable accommodation, lagoon views, pine forests, spa, pools and a beach shuttle.

Budget

Yacht Classic Hotel, 1 Karagözler No 24, 48300 Fethiye, tel: 252 612 5067, www.yachtclassichotel.com Sleek little boutique hotel beside the harbour; restaurant, bar, pool and *hamam*.

Kalkan

Luxury

Kalkan Regency Hotel, tel: +44 20 8605 3500, www.exclusiveescapes.co.uk Sybaritic retreat, with great views and food, part of the luscious Exclusive Escapes chain that dots the south coast with some of the Mediterranean's most romantic small hotels.

Lykia Residence and Spa, Yalboyu Mah. Akdeniz Caddesi, Smbl Sokak, No. 1, tel: 242 844 1055, www.likyakalkan.com Swish 5-star resort and spa, 15 mins walk from town; shuttle to its private beach club. Fabulous views and great food.

Budget

Lizo Hotel, Milli Egemenlik Caddesi, Kalamar Yolu 57, Pk 110, Kalkan, tel: 242 844 3381, http://lizohotel.com Pretty, friendly family hotel behind the town, with restaurant, bar, garden, and pool.

Kaş

Mid-range

Nur Beach Hotel, Küçük Çakıl Mah. 45, tel: 242 836 1828, www.nurbeachhotel.com Delightfully restored Ottoman house; beach bar, excellent restaurant, private beach and simple but beautiful rooms.

Budget

Hideaway Hotel, Eski Kilise Sok. No 7, Kaş Merkez, Kaş 07580, tel: 242 836 1887, www.hotelhideaway.com Charming little (20-room) hotel with terrace restaurant set amidst olive trees. Sea views and pool.

Antalya

Mid-range

Rixos Downtown Antalya, Sakıp Sabancı Bulvarı, Konyaaltı Sahili, 07050 Antalya, tel: 242 249 4949, www.rixos.com/en/rixos-downtown-antalya-hotel The former Sheraton now headed slightly downmarket but still an extremely good business and tourist hotel superbly located on the seafront near the museum.

Minyon Hotel, Kılınçaslan mah. Tabakhane sok. No 31, Kaleiçi, tel: 242 247 11 47, www.minyonhotel.com Old town mansion beautifully restored and furnished with

antiques. Six rooms, plunge pool, lovely gardens and views.
Alp Paşa Hotel, Barbaros Mahallesi, Hesapçı Sokak 30–32, Kaleiçi, Antalya, tel: 242 247 5676, fax: 242 248 5074, www.alppasa.com Traditional caravanserai style.

Budget

Otantic Butik Otel, Barbaros Mahallesi Hesapçi Sok. 14, Kaleiçi, tel: 242 244 8530, www.otantikbutikotel.com/eng Restored Ottoman mansion in the heart of the old town with its own bar, excellent restaurant and a lovely courtyard.

Belek

Luxury

Ela Quality Resort, Īskele Mevkii, Belek, tel: 242 710 2200, www.elaresort.com One of the finest of many five-star resorts gracing this up-market golfing village near Antalya.

Where to Eat

Marmaris

Ney, Castle Street, tel: 252 412 021. Tiny backstreet gem serving authentic Turkish cuisine. Good wine list and views. Get there early for a rooftop or window table.
The Drunken Crab, 53a Bar St, tel: 252 412 3970, www.drunkencrabrestaurant.com Tiny town centre favourite serving meze and seafood. Open Apr–Oct.

Kalkan

Belgin's Kitchen, Yaliboyu Mah, tel: 242 844 3614. Ottoman cuisine, in sybaritic luxury. Summer only.

Kaş

Bahçe, top of main shopping street, opposite sarcophagus, tel: 242 836 2370. Imaginative food. Booking essential.
Ratatouille, Cumhuriyet Meydanı, Kaş 07560, tel: 531 724 5846. Upstairs restaurant, just off the main square, serving scrumptious Turkish food and international haute cuisine.

Ulupınar

Ristorante Kayalar, Ulupınar Koyu Merkez Mah, tel: 242 825 0010. Just one of many hugely popular fresh trout restaurants in the mountains near Olympos.

Antalya

Seraser Fine Dining Restaurant, Tuzcular mah. Karanlik sok. No 18, Kaleici, Antalya 07100, tel: 242 247 6015, www.seraserrestaurant.com Delicious international haute cuisine in an elegant old town setting. Outdoor terrace.
Lal Café, Iskele Cad. 5, Kaleiçi, tel: 242 244 6236. Laid-back outdoor harbour café, perfect for lazy lunches and whiling away sunny afternoons.

Aksu

Anadolu Park, Serik Caddesi, Konak Mh. Aksu Çıkısı, Aksu, tel: 242 426 2400. Huge (and hugely popular) country restaurant near the airport, serving brunch, full meals and barbecue kits.

Alanya

Red Tower Brewery, Iskele Caddesi 80, Alanya, tel: 242 513 6664, www.redtowerbrewery.com Six floors of harbourside entertainment with its own microbrewery, restaurant, sports bar and sky lounge – there's something for everyone.

Fethiye

Sarnic, Eski Cesme Sokak No 57, Kayaköy, tel: 252 618 0153. Entrancing garden restaurant in the deserted village. Hugely romantic – and the traditional Turkish food is mouthwateringly good.

Tours and Excursions

Most hotels arrange excursions and **yacht charter**. Try a day trip by *gulet* to **classical sites** or charter a boat.
Bougainville Travel, Ibrahim Serin Cad 10, Kaş 07580, tel: 242 836 3737. Cultural tours. Diving for the disabled, www.bougainville-turkey.com
Inshore Travel, Sarı ana mah. 20. Sok. 1 oral apart, Marmaris, tel: 252 412 5016/7, www.inshoretravel.com

Useful Contacts

Tourist Information:
Marmaris, Iskele Meydanı, tel: 252 412 1035.
Fethiye, Iskele Meydanı, tel: 252 614 1527.
Kaş, Cumhuriyet Meydanı 5, tel: 242 836 1238.
Antalya, Cumhuriyet Caddesi, tel: 242 241 1747.
Turkish Airlines: 24-hour central reservations, tel: 212 444 0849, www.thy.com.tr
Aspendos Opera and Ballet Festival: tel: 242 243 7640, www.aspendosfestival.gov.tr

6
The Heart of Anatolia

Paradoxically, the most prominent feature of the ancient Turkish centre of Anatolia is modern-day **Ankara**, which was chosen as the country's capital by Atatürk in the 1920s.

Ankara may appear somewhat soulless and cold in its modernity, yet it treasures its history and the **Museum of Anatolian Civilizations** contains the greatest collection of Hittite relics in the world.

At the major **Hittite sites,** east of Ankara, you can see the impressive 3000-year-old ruins of an enigmatic civilization, the cities and holy places of an empire which dared to challenge the mighty ancient Egyptians in battle, in the very first 'world war', over 1000 years before the birth of Christ.

Further to the south lies the haunting region of **Cappadocia**. No similar architecture or lifestyle existed anywhere else. The amazing conical dwellings, underground cities and devotional churches are a chilling revelation of a prehistoric ghetto lifestyle. Very little of this extraordinary life is documented. It is all left to the imagination.

The capital of Cappadocia is the traditional city of **Kayseri**, which boasts one of the largest ancient bazaars in the country, as well as a 700-year-old mosque. Directly south of Ankara lies the Muslim holy city of **Konya**, once the home of the famous Order of **Whirling Dervishes**. This fascinating ritual ceremony, whose every movement has deep spiritual significance, is performed every year in December.

Don't Miss

*** **Cappadocia:** eerie landscape of wind-sculpted rock and underground cities.
*** **Konya:** home of the famous Whirling Dervishes.
** **Ankara:** the nation's capital, site of the **Museum of Anatolian Civilizations**, containing the world's finest collection of Hittite relics.
** **The Hittite sites:** ruins of a mysterious 3000-year-old empire.
** **Kayseri:** has one of the finest bazaars in the land.

◀ *Opposite: Kayseri has one of the largest ancient bazaars in the country.*

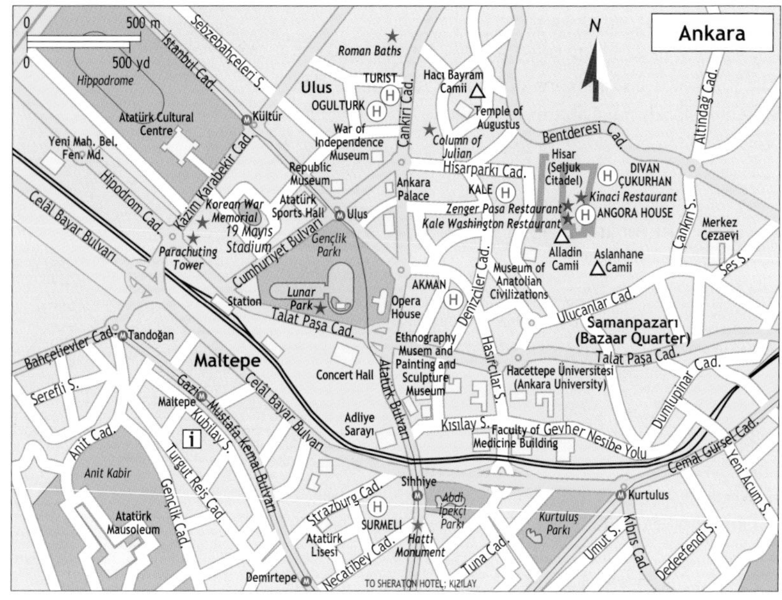

ANKARA

In Roman times, Ankara was little more than a small sheep-farming town. The sheep of Anatolia were famous for their **Angora** wool and the word 'Angora' is, in fact, simply a corruption of the town's name.

When Atatürk became president, he chose Ankara as his new capital. At the time it was a provincial backwater with a population of less than 30,000. It had no pavements, electricity, or covered sewers. Atatürk, determined to westernize, commissioned German architect Hermann Jansen, 'the man who built modern Berlin', to build him a new capital.

Modern Ankara lies in the very heart of Anatolia, approximately 425km (265 miles) to the east of Istanbul. It now has a population of around five million people, but has none of the exotic splendour of the former capital, Istanbul. Nevertheless, its citizens prefer it this way. For them, Ankara projects the modern, forward-looking face of Turkey.

CLIMATE

Summer in this region is not as hot as elsewhere in Turkey, and the lack of humidity makes it feel much **fresher** than on the coast. **Spring** and **autumn** too, are **cooler**, but winter can be severe, with midday temperatures remaining below zero.

The Old Town and Citadel ★★

A kilometre or so north of the modern town centre you can still see a few remains of Roman Ankara. In **Ulus Meydani** stands the **Column of Julian**, which was erected in the 4th century AD, to mark a visit by the Emperor Julian the Apostate. Northeast of here, the **Hacı Bayram Camii** (the city's main mosque) stands amid the ruins of the **Temple of Augustus**. Not much is left of this building, apart from the walls which date from the 2nd century BC, when they were erected by the King of Pergamon. Northwest of here, back across Çankir Caddesi, you can still distinguish the outline and ducts of the **Roman Baths**.

East of Roman Ankara, at the end of **Hisarparkı Caddesi**, you come to the **Seljuk Citadel** (Hisar), whose original walls were built by the Byzantines. Beyond the impressive gateway lie the twisting narrow streets and wooden houses of Ottoman Ankara. From the northern end of the Citadel, at Ak Kale, there's a fine view out over the city. The **Alladin Camii**, at the southern end of the Citadel, dates from the 12th-century Seljuk period. South of here you come to the **Bazaar quarter**, where Angora wool is still sold. In the midst of this district stands the oldest and most imposing Seljuk mosque, the 13th-century **Aslanhane Camii**. Inside there is an ornate wooden ceiling, supported by lines of wooden columns. The mosque is named after the Stone Lion in the courtyard (*Aslanhane* means 'lion house' in Turkish).

Beside the entrance to the citadel, a former Caravanserai, the Çengel Han, has been transformed into the splendid **Rahmi M. Koç Museum**, with an eclectic selection of toys, transport and other collectibles.

Museum of Anatolian Civilizations ★★

Some 300m (985ft) east of Aslanhane Camii is the Museum of Anatolian Civilizations. It is the most interesting spot in Ankara, and houses the greatest collection of **Hittite antiquities** in the world. The Hittite civilization flourished in Anatolia during

A Roman Mistake

When the Ancient Romans occupied Ankara, they thought its name was the Greek word for anchor. The new coins they minted here proudly displayed an anchor on the back as an emblem for the city. Regrettably, Ankara is over 200km (125 miles) from the sea, which caused great mirth among its citizens. The Romans, who were not renowned for their sense of humour, failed to see the joke. Even when their mistake was pointed out to them, they refused to change the city's emblem.

▼ *Below: Kite-flyers enjoy themselves on the topmost wall of the castle at Ankara.*

King Midas

In the 7th century BC Midas was the ruler of Phrygia, the kingdom traversed by the trade routes between Greece and the Middle East. He accumulated huge revenues from the caravans that passed through his territory, eventually becoming the richest ruler in Asia Minor, which led to the legend that everything he touched turned to gold. We still speak of 'the Midas touch'.

the second millennium BC, and for a while their empire almost rivalled that of ancient Egypt. The fascinating relics and statues conjure up an intriguing picture of a civilization about which very little is known. Be sure to see the curiously evocative exhibit of the mother goddesses, some as old as 8000 years, which are thought to have acted as fertility symbols. Open daily Apr–Oct 08:30–19:00, Nov–Mar 08:30–17:30.

Atatürk Mausoleum (Anıtkabir) ★★

No visit to Ankara would be complete without a visit to the Atatürk Mausoleum. Few leaders left such an enduring symbol of immortality. Open daily Apr–Oct 09:00–17:00, Nov–Mar 09:00–16:00. The museum closes from 12:00–13:00. There are sound and light shows on some evenings (check locally for details).

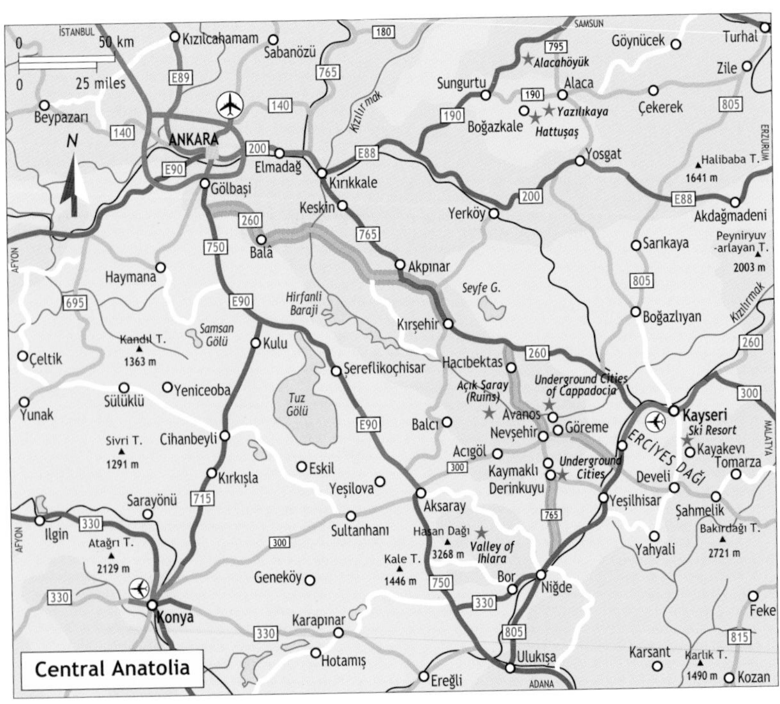

HITTITE SITES

▲ *Above: The Aslanlıkapı, or Lion Gate, forms the main entrance to Hattuşaş, the Hittite capital.*

References to the Hittites are made in both the Old Testament and in ancient Egyptian records. They arrived in Anatolia during the second millennium BC, yet, even today our knowledge of this great empire is still very sketchy. Unlike the Babylonians and the ancient Egyptians, Hittite civilization was not in fact centred around the fertile valley of a great river, but took the form of a highland existence. The Hittite Empire lasted for over 1000 years, and then vanished as mysteriously as it had begun.

Hattuşaş ★★

The main Hittite sites lie 120km (75 miles) east of Ankara. **Hattuşaş** was the capital of the Hittite Empire and even today its ruins cover a large area. A circuit of the site follows the 6km (4 miles) of city walls and will take you around two hours. The walk leads you to the **Great Temple**, the impressive **Lion Gate** (whose flanking lions are replicas, the originals having been moved to Ankara), the Sphinx and King's Gates, and the **Great Fortress** which was the residence of the kings and was approached by a ramp. Open 08:00–12:00, 13:00–17:30 daily .

Other Hittite Sites ★

About 3km (2 miles) east of Hattuşaş lies **Yazılıkaya**, the religious centre of the Hittite Empire, with its large ruined temple. Some 24km (15 miles) north of here is **Alacahöyük**, where there's a fine **Sphinx Gate**, a relief of a royal procession, and a secret tunnel whose purpose remains a mystery. The **royal tombs** here have been extensively excavated (all the finds are on display in Ankara). There's also a small **museum**, which contains a Hittite bath. Open 08:00–12:00 and 13:00–17:30 daily.

Ancient Ankara

Contrary to its modern appearance, Ankara has been inhabited for centuries. The city was founded in the 7th century BC by the legendary **King Midas**, whose touch turned everything to gold. In early Christian times the city was part of the Roman province of **Galatia** and was visited by **St Paul**, who founded a church here. When St Paul continued on his travels, he wrote to the Christians he had left behind in Ankara. His letter appears in the Bible as the 'Epistle to the Galatians'.

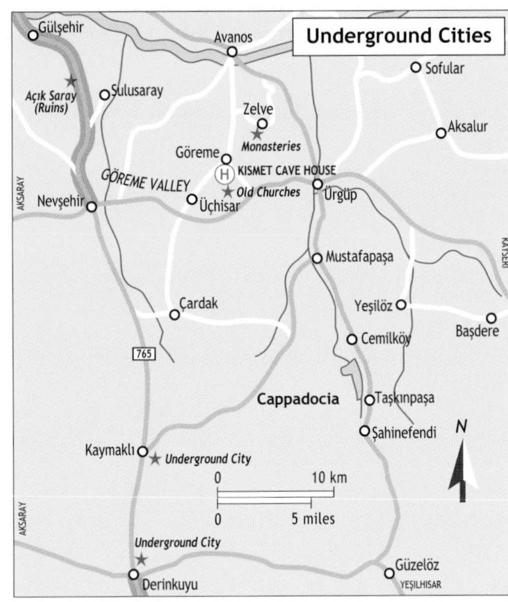

CAPPADOCIA

Cappadocia lies about 180km (110 miles) southeast of Ankara. This region of soft volcanic rock has been sculpted into pillars and columns of fantastic shapes by many centuries of wind, snow, rain and erosion. The pliable rock was further changed by human hands, resulting in a stunning variety of **caves** and **underground cities**.

The Hittites were the first people who lived in this area, but rock-carving began here in earnest only after Greek and Armenian **Christian hermits** arrived in the 4th century. Cappadocia then became one of the most important early Christian centres in the eastern Mediterranean. Even after Cappadocia was conquered by Muslims in the 11th century, the Christians here were left largely undisturbed. Today tourism centres around the villages of Göreme, Üchisar and Ürgup.

Why Live Underground?

Soon after the early Christians settled in Cappadocia, they began to suffer from Arab raids. After the death of Mohammed in AD632, Muslim Arabs from Arabia had begun expanding throughout the Middle East and North Africa. The Christians of Cappadocia found themselves increasingly vulnerable and defenceless, so they decided to disappear underground, leaving no signs of life. The ruse worked. When the Arab attackers arrived, they found no towns or villages. The valleys among the rock faces appeared to be utterly deserted.

Göreme ★★★

Göreme has a superb open-air museum (open daily Apr–Oct 08:00–19:00, Nov–Mar 08:00–17:00). The rock chapels here date from around the 10th to the 13th century – the Byzantine and Seljuk periods. The most spectacular of all are the **Karanlık Kilise** (Dark Church), with its splendidly preserved frescoes of Christ and Judas, the **Elmalı Kilise** (Apple Church), and the **Tokalı Kilise** (Buckle Church), the largest of them all, which even features a small chapel downstairs. The nearby valleys, filled with weird rock formations, are honeycombed with fascinating but eerie troglodite dwellings.

A few kilometres north of Göreme lies **Zelve**, with three valleys of abandoned, concealed **monasteries** carved into the rock, some of which date back to the 8th century, possibly even earlier. Approximately 8km (5 miles) north of here you come to the pleasant riverside town of **Avanos**, which is famous for its **pottery** and more underground caverns.

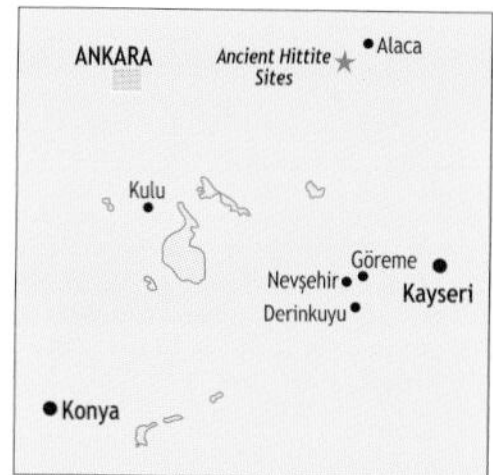

Derinkuyu ★★★

About 25km (15 miles) south of Göreme lies a truly spectacular, many-layered **underground city** (none of which is visible above the surface). Each tier is a labyrinth of tunnels, with living quarters for humans and animals, as well as wine cellars, bakeries and ventilation shafts. You may explore, but it becomes claustrophobic the deeper you go and few reach the bottom.

Another most intriguing underground city lies just to the north of Derinkuyu at **Kaymaklı**. This maze of tunnels and chambers is even more intricate and apparently haphazard. Be sure to follow the arrows which lead you through, otherwise it's not easy to find your way out again. Both open daily 08:00–17:00 year-round.

Cappadocia's Volcanic Past

The entire region of Cappadocia is covered with outcrops of volcanic rock. These are all that remain of the massive lava flows from a nearby volcano which was active during prehistoric times. Nowadays, snow-capped **Mt Erciyes** is extinct, and its peak can be seen, rising to nearly 4000m (13,100ft) to the south of Cappadocia.

Valley of Ihlara ★★

Approximately 32km (20 miles) west of Derinkuyu lies the 10km (6-mile) Ihlara Valley, used as a retreat by Byzantine monks 1000 years ago. A dozen of their many churches and chapels are open to the public, carved into the rocks or built out of local stone. Among the best are the **Church of the Snakes** and the **Church of the Hyacinths**.

This valley is dominated by the high cone of **Hasan Dağı**, a dormant volcano which still emits a plume of smoke from time to time.

▼ *Below: The eerie rock dwellings of Cappadocia.*

KAYSERI

Kayseri lies beneath snow-clad Mt Erciyes, an extinct volcano that has been developed as a **skiing** centre.

Many curious **Seljuk tombs** are scattered throughout the city, the most ornate of which is the 13th-century **Döner Kümbet**, in the centre of a traffic circle close to the Archaeological Museum. The main mosque is the impressive 13th-century **Ulu Camii** (Great Mosque), which took over 100 years to complete. In the **bazaar** quarter good buys are gold jewellery, carpets and kilims.

KONYA

Konya is home to the **Whirling Dervishes**, founded by the *sufi* (Muslim sage) Mevlâna in the 13th century. This holy place has been inhabited for almost 7000 years, and Hittite remains (now in Ankara) were found in **Alâeddin Park,** just west of the city centre. Here you can also see the 12th-century **Alâeddin Mosque**. Its odd shape was dictated by the building materials (stones and columns pinched from nearby Roman ruins).

The Whirling Dervishes

Although this religious order was disbanded by Atatürk in the 1920s, their ritual dance is today re-enacted in a ceremony which takes place annually in December. The costumes of the dancers, and each of their movements, have a specific meaning: the black capes symbolize the darkness of the grave; the shedding of these capes during the dance signifies the dancers' escape from the tomb and the imprisonment of the flesh; the white robes represent shrouds, and their conical hats denote the gravestones. There are regular tourist displays in summer; details from Konya Tourist Office.

Mevlâna Museum ★★★

The tombs of Mevlâna and many of his most illustrious followers are on view at the Mevlâna Museum. This is also a **shrine** and a destination of pilgrimage – so you must be appropriately dressed and remove your shoes before entering the tombs. Women's heads and bare arms must be covered and shorts are not allowed. Open daily 09:00–17:30.

▼ *Below: In action, the Whirling Dervishes of Konya are a truly extraordinary sight.*

Karatay Medrese ★★

The **Karatay Museum,** 1km (½ mile) west of here, has superb ceramics and tiles. The awe-inspiring **Dome of Stars** is lined with beautiful Seljuk tiles. At its base is an inscription from the first chapter of the Koran. Open 08:30–12:00, 13:30–17:30, closed Mondays.

Best Times to Visit

Ankara can be very hot in July and August. Winter can be very cold. Best time to visit is **early summer** or **autumn**.

Getting There

Ankara's Esenboğa Airport has regular flights to all the major European destinations. It also offers regular internal flights to all the main cities in Turkey. The train to Istanbul is being updated to a hi-speed line.

Where to Stay

Ankara

Luxury

Divan Çukurhan, Tarihi Ankara Kalesi Necatibey Mahallesi Depo Sokak No 3, Ulus, tel: 312 306 6400, www.divan.com.tr Wonderful old caravanserai now restored as a fabulously chic boutique hotel.

Angora House Hotel, Kalekapisi Sokak 16–18, Ulus & Citadel, tel: 312 309 8380, fax: 312 309 8381. Delightful little hotel in restored citadel house. Booking essential.

Göreme

Budget

Kookaburra Pension, Pos. Codu, 50180 Göreme, tel: 384 271 2549, http://kookaburramotel.com All charm and hospitality with rounded doors and cave rooms. Enchanting.

Kismet Cave House, Kağnı yolu 9, Göreme, tel: 384 271 2416, www.kismetcavehouse.com Delightful. Eight rooms.

Konya

Mid-range

Hilton Garden Inn, Aziziye Mahallesi, Kislaonu Sokak 4, Konya 42030, tel: 332 221 6000, http://hiltongardeninn3.hilton.com Comfortable chain hotel; good service and breakfast buffet; about 20 mins walk from the Mevlana Museum.

Üçhisar (Nevşehir)

Mid-range

Les Maisons de Cappadoce, Belediye Meyd. 24, tel/fax: 384 219 2782, www.cappadoce.com Twelve restored cave houses, in various sizes. All with kitchens, gardens and fabulous views.

Ürgüp

Mid-range

Ürgüp Evi Cave Hotel, Esbelli Mah. 54, tel: 384 341 3173, www.urgupevi.com.tr Award-winning small hotel cut into the caves of Cappadocia. The food is also excellent.

Where to Eat

Ankara

Trilye, Hafta Sokak No 11/B, Gaziosmanpaşa, tel: 312 447 1200, www.trilye.com.tr Sumptuous and imaginative seafood restaurant with romantic gardens. Ankara's favourite society hotspot. Not cheap but definitely worth it.

Kale Washington, Doyuran Sokak 5/7, Kaleiçi, tel: 312 311 4344. This is a restored Ottoman mansion in the citadel; serves fine food; a terrace used in summer.

Tours and Excursions

Most hotels in the area arrange day trips to the rock caves. Cappadocia is 2–3 hours from Ankara; many agencies arrange tours. Cars are best, but tour options include hiking, mountain biking, horseback and hot-air balloon excursions.

Tour and Travel Agents:

Middle Earth Travel, Gaferli Mah Cevizler Sokak 20, 50180 Göreme, tel: 384 271 2559, www.middleearthtravel.com Excellent tour company, based in Cappadocia, offering hiking and climbing as well as local tours and sightseeing.

Useful Contacts

Tourism Information:

Ankara, Gazi Mustafa Kemal Bulvarı 121, Maltepe, tel: 312 231 5572.

Esenboğa Airport, Ankara, tel: 312 398 0348.

Ürgüp, Park Içi, tel: 384 341 4059.

Turkish Airlines: Ankara, tel: 312 428 0200, fax: 312 428 1681, 24-hour central reservations tel: 212 444 0849, www.thy.com.tr

ANKARA	J	F	M	A	M	J	J	A	S	O	N	D
AVERAGE TEMP. °F	34	30	51	63	73	78	86	87	78	69	57	40
AVERAGE TEMP. °C	1	-1	11	17	23	26	30	31	26	21	14	4
RAINFALL in	1	1	1	1	2	1	1	1	1	1	1	2
RAINFALL mm	33	31	33	33	48	25	13	10	18	23	31	48
DAYS OF RAINFALL	8	8	7	7	7	5	2	1	3	5	6	9

7
The Black Sea Coast

The Black Sea coast region is one of Turkey's undiscovered pleasures. The first surprise is how lush and green it is here. The mountains often rise steeply from the sea, making for the most breathtaking coastal scenery.

Jason and the Argonauts travelled along these shores in their quest for the Golden Fleece. This was also the home of the legendary Amazons (*see* page 105), a fierce tribe of female warriors.

A motorway now runs most of the length of the Black Sea coast but you whizz past coastal villages, sea views and hinterland, which were linked via the old road. To really appreciate the charm of the region, rent a car in one of the main cities and explore the hamlets at leisure.

Sinop is the oldest and most attractive of the coastal cities. Further east you come to **Samsun**, an industrial port and centre of the tobacco industry. Inland from here you can visit **Amasya**, a delightful small mountain town with many ancient mosques and a number of historic buildings. Travelling east from Samsun, you reach several small resorts, the best of which is **Ünye**. However, the most exotic destination in this region is undoubtedly **Trabzon**, which for a brief period was the far-flung capital of the Byzantine empire. Inland from here lies the spectacular **Sumela Monastery**. High in the mountains, this is the most distant, but also the most spectacular sight in the area.

Don't Miss

***** Sumela:** spectacular ancient monastery high in the mountains.
***** Sinop:** historic city with a picturesque harbour, beaches and classical sites.
**** Trabzon:** romantic city made famous by Rose Macauley's book *The Towers of Trebizond.*
**** Amasya:** historic, unspoilt inland town.

◀ *Opposite: Tea plantations alternate with almond trees in blossom along the fertile Black Sea Coast.*

SAFRANBOLU

A short distance inland, Safranbolu was a popular and prosperous trading centre, famous for spice, leather and

Classic Paranoid

Sinop was the home of one of the most notorious kings of classical times. **Mithradates Eupator** was the paranoid ruler of the Pontic Empire, which covered most of north-western Anatolia in the 2nd century BC. He locked his mother in a dungeon, and then married his sister, by whom he had several sons. But evidently family life didn't agree with him, so he murdered them all. Later he decided to declare war on the Roman Empire and, after slaughtering 80,000 Roman citizens and driving the rest out of Anatolia, he thought he had won. But the Romans returned in even greater numbers. Mithradates Eupator was defeated, tried to poison himself and when this failed, ordered his body-guard to run him through with his sword.

metalwork. The town's magnificent collection of restored 19th-century **Ottoman houses** merit UNESCO World Heritage. At the heart of the old quarter, **Yemeniciler Arastası** is the original leather workers' bazaar and still an excellent shopping stop. Individual houses worth a visit include the old **Governor's Residence**, now the **Kaymakamlar Müzesi** (open daily 08:30–12:30 and 13:30–17:30), the huge 17th-century **Cincihanı Caravansaray**, **Köprülü Mehmet Paşa Camii**, and the restored Ottoman **Cinci Hamam** (bath house).

About 5km outside Safranbolu, the **Mencilis (Bulak) Caves** are the fourth largest in Turkey with magnificent stalactite formations and an underground river (check locally for tours). From here, the coast road heads east through the beautiful town of **Amasra**, with Hellenistic and Roman remains, Byzantine walls and Ottoman houses.

SINOP

Sinop, situated on an isthmus, is the most charming city on the Black Sea coast. It has a lovely harbour, beaches, classical sites and a lively summer nightlife.

The walled city is named after the Amazon **queen Sinope**, who evaded the designs of the lusty god Zeus by tricking him into granting her eternal virginity. Sinop was also the home of **Diogenes**, the famous Greek Cynic philosopher who rejected social standards and lived in a barrel. When Alexander the Great passed through here in the 4th century BC, he called on Diogenes, who was sunbathing outside his barrel. Alexander was so impressed by Diogenes' carefree lifestyle that he offered the philosopher whatever he wished. Diogenes replied: 'Could you step out of the way, you're blocking the sun'. There has been a fortress here since the 7th century BC and everyone from the Persians to the Byzantines and the Seljuks had a hand in its construction but most of what you see now is Ottoman, dating back around 500 years. The city also has a museum, a 13th-century mosque, 7th-century church with intriguing finds dating from the classical era, the remains of the **Temple of Serapis** (an Egyptian god, better known as Apollo), and the former prison, which has bizarrely become a tourism sight.

To the west of Sinop the delightfully scenic coastal road passes through a long series of villages, with mostly empty beaches. The coastline here remains largely unspoilt and is only visited in summer, mainly by locals. East of Sinop, tiny Gerza is delightful. It is untouched by tourism, but does have a few small motels.

CLIMATE

The Black Sea coast is **temperate**, compared to the rest of the country. This means that summers are not too hot, with temperatures around 25°C (77°F). The only drawback is that it rains often, which can make this region seem a bit dismal during the colder seasons, even though the temperature doesn't fall below 10°C (50°F).

SAMSUN

This sprawling industrial city is the largest port on the Black Sea coast, and a centre of the **tobacco** industry. There's little here in the way of tourist attractions, but it has useful ferry connections to Istanbul and Trabzon during the summer.

It was at Samsun that Atatürk launched the **Turkish War of Independence** after the Greeks invaded at the end of World War I, an event that marked the inception of modern Turkey.

If you are spending time in Samsun, be sure to visit the local **museum**. The collection of relics reflects the city's long history, which began over 26 centuries ago. It's also well worth walking around the busy port area, which has an atmospheric market where you can buy a wide variety of Soviet mementoes from itinerant Russian traders. It also

▼ *Below: Though heavily industrialized, Samsun retains some atmospheric old buildings.*

The Original Cherry

The Romans first colonized this remote stretch of coast in the 1st century BC. They called the town we now know as Giresun, Cerasus. Here they discovered a luscious little fruit, growing on trees they had not seen before. This was the cherry, which had arrived on the Black Sea coast some centuries previously from China. The Romans soon began exporting *cerasus* to Europe, naming it after the town of its origin. Our word, cherry, is a corruption of the Roman name.

has a replica of Ataturk's ship, the *SS Bandırma*, of the great man himself and his followers. Near the town, the Kızılırmak Delta is a hugely important birding area with around 320 species spotted there.

AMASYA

This historic mountain town lies approximately 125km (80 miles) south of Samsun in the picturesque valley of the Yeşil Irmak (Green River) and has remained largely unspoilt. The town itself has several fine mosques. The **Gümüslü Cami** (Silver Mosque) dates from the 13th century. Even older is the **Burmalı Minare Cami** (Mosque of the Twisted Minaret) – though the interesting twisting effect lies in the spiralling stonework, rather than in the structure itself. But perhaps the best thing about Amasya is its timless provincial atmosphere. This is the Turkey very few visitors get to see. Walk around the streets and see the many ancient buildings which include such oddities as a 400-year-old Ottoman lunatic asylum.

Tombs of the Pontic Kings ★

On the north bank of the river, a number of paths lead up the hillside to a cliff above the town, where several large tombs were carved into the rock, some

▼ *Below: Some of the tombs carved into the rock face above Amasya date back more than 2000 years.*

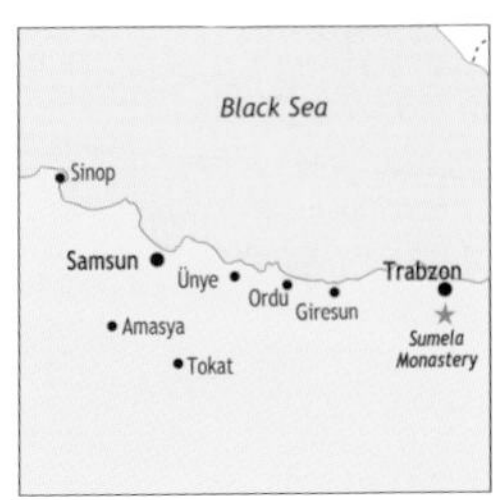

◀ *Left: Many of the beaches along the Black Sea coast have barely been touched by tourism.*

over 2000 years ago. Nearby is the so-called Palace of the Maidens, where local pashas once kept their harems. Below the tombs is an old quarter consisting of charming, wooden Ottoman houses. One of these, **Hazeranlar Konağı**, has been beautifully restored and now houses a small local **ethnology museum**. Open 09:00–12:30 and 13:30–17:30 Tuesday–Sunday.

The only way to the **citadel** is along the road leading northeast past **Büyük Ağa Medresesi**, a 15th-century seminary. Fine views from the top sweep over the town and the remains of the Pontic Fort.

GIRESUN

This sleepy town lies just 130km (80 miles) west down the road from Ünye. The coastal ferry calls in here, and the main point of interest is **Giresun Adası**, an island 6km (4 miles) offshore. In prehistoric times this island was called Aretias, and was the home of the much-feared **Amazons**, a fierce tribe of female warriors. During the Byzantine era the monastery of St Phocas, whose ruins can still be seen, was established here.

According to tradition, the curiously pagan **Giresun-Aksu Festival** takes place around the island on 20 May each year. Locals encircle it with their boats, each throwing a pebble into the water and making a wish. This gesture is followed by wild celebrations.

Back in town, the most pleasant spot is the **Kalepark** around the castle, which is still surprisingly rural and is a good place for a picnic.

The Amazons

According to legend, the Amazons, who crop up in several of the Greek myths, and are also mentioned in Homer's *Iliad*, arrived on the Black Sea coast in prehistoric times from India. They were a fierce tribe of warrior women, distinguished by the intriguing fact that they each had only one breast. They are said to have cut off their right breast, because it got in the way of their bow-strings, and also impeded their javelin-throwing. The Amazons were a strictly female community. Once every year a group of them would set out and round up a few promising males from nearby tribes, so that the Amazons could produce offspring. Only female offspring were allowed to remain members of the tribe.

Whilst hazelnut production dominates the local economy in much of this area, Giresun and Ordu are two of the few remaining outposts of handcrafted gun production. This traditional industry is still carried on by several local firms. Hand guns are meticulously made and often elaborately decorated and inlaid with mother-of-pearl by local craftsmen (*usta* in Turkish). Many are sought after as collectors' items.

TRABZON

For centuries, the former Trebizond was regarded throughout Europe as one of the most romantic cities of the East. It constituted the Black Sea end of the fabled Silk Route, which brought rare oriental goods and spices all the way across Asia from China. For a brief period during the 13th century, the city was even the capital of the Byzantine Empire.

Today's Trabzon is a bustling commercial port squeezed between the mountains and the sea. It has several interesting sights dating from its moment of historical greatness. These include a number of ruined Byzantine churches, as well as the tumbledown remains of the palace which once ruled an empire.

The town itself has a lively **market** and interesting port area. Until well into this century camel caravans would leave the Meydanı (city's main square) carrying pilgrims on the long trek across the Levant to Mecca. (These now travel by bus from the old camel stables.)

The Trapezuntine Empire

In 1204, after the sacking of Constantinople, Trebizond was briefly established as the capital of the Byzantine empire – which consequently became known as the Trapezuntine Empire. During this period, the name of the city became a byword for 'Byzantine intrigue', as its rulers sought to cling on to their crumbling realm. In order to appease the Mongol invaders from the east, they even sold off their daughters to Mongol chieftains. Trebizond's respectability was finally re-established by Rose Macauley's marvellous novel *The Towers of Trebizond*.

The Bazaar ★★

Ten minutes' walk east of the Meydanı you reach the bustling **Bazaar quarter**. Here you can buy anything from cheap ballpoint pens to live rabbits (for the pot, rather than as pets). More interesting for souvenirs is the port quarter, just northeast of the Meydanı.

Proximity to Russia has altered shopping patterns. Turks and Russians excel at flamboyant, freewheeling trade and bargaining adds the final flourish. Anything marketable can be found in the bazaar.

Ortahisar ★

A 10-minute walk up the hill southwest of the main Bazaar brings you to **Ortahisar** (Middle Castle**)**, a district of winding streets and old houses occupying the old fortified Citadel. **Ortahisar Camii**, just inside the northwest walls, is now the main mosque. The building dates from the 13th century, and was once the main Orthodox cathedral of the Trapezuntine Empire. At the southern end of Ortahisar are the remains of the Byzantine Palace, from which the emperors ruled their ramshackle empire.

Aya Sofia ★

Roughly 3km (2 miles) west of the Meydanı you come to the local Aya Sofia, which dates from the 13th century. This ruined building displays an odd blend of Seljuk and Byzantine influences. The showpieces here are the recently restored late-Byzantine **frescoes**, which somehow survived the Ottoman period when the building was used as an ammunition dump.

Atatürk's Villa ★★

About 5km (3 miles) west of town and reachable by regular bus and dolmuş service from the Meydanı lies Atatürk's villa. It was built at the turn of the century for a Greek banker, and is a rare example of the Crimean style. Atatürk stayed here several times, and the villa now houses an exhibition of his personal mementoes, including some interesting old photos and annotated maps of his campaigns. Open 08:30–16:30 daily.

Artvin

East of Trabzon, the far northeast of Turkey is more culturally attuned to Georgia and Armenia than to the rest of Turkey – this was once the centre of the Armenian kingdom. There are several high ranges of mountains, including the Kaçkars, where Ayder has become a centre for climbing, hiking and eco-holidays. Artvin itself and its surrounding villages has some spectacular 9th–11th-century churches including former monasteries at Işhan, Hahuli and Öşk Vank. The local Kafkasor Festival is a colourful event that includes bull fighting (between bulls).

◀ *Opposite: Atatürk's villa outside Trabzon is now an interesting museum.*

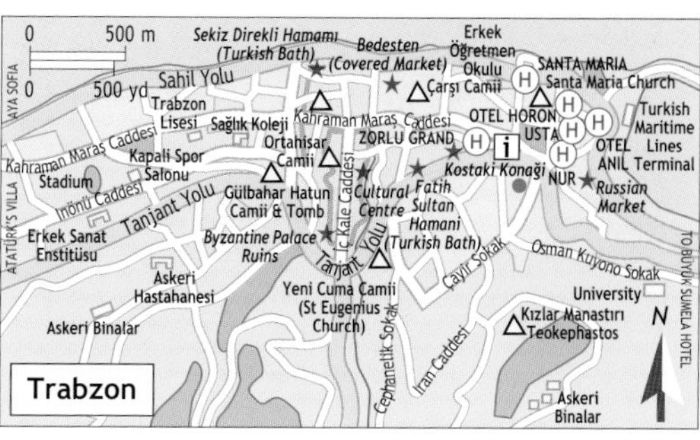

The Miraculous Icon

When Greek Orthodox monks were forced to leave the monastery at Sumela in the 1920s, they were forbidden to take anything with them. Before they left, the monks hid as many of the monastery's treasures as they could. The miraculous icon of the Virgin, which was said to have been painted by St Luke, was secretly buried in the nearby mountains. Ten years later a Greek Orthodox monk made his way back to the site disguised as a goatherd, and dug it up. He managed to smuggle it out of the country, and took it to Athens, where the icon is now on display at the Benaki Museum.

SUMELA

Some 50km (30 miles) south of Trabzon, high in the mountains amid the fir trees and mist, lies the spectacular Monastery of the Black Virgin of Sumela. According to legend, it was founded in the 4th century by a Greek monk called Barabas, who had been led to this remote spot by a sacred icon of the Virgin Mary. The image, said to have been painted by St Luke, was renowned for its miraculous powers.

For many centuries this monastery was one of the holy centres of the Byzantine Church, and was even visited by Ottoman sultans as a mark of respect. It flourished until the early 20th century, when its monks were shipped back to Greece after the Graeco–Turkish conflict that followed World War I. The ruined monastery and superb frescoes have recently been restored. It is reached by way of a 40-minute walk up a steep mountain track, which affords spectacular views across the gorge and down the wooded valley.

While you walk up, you see the monastery clinging to the sheer rock face high above you. There is something almost Tibetan in its remote fastness and inaccessibility, curiously echoed by its cliff-hanging external architecture beneath the rock face and the circling eagles above. Open Tue–Sun Apr–Oct 09:00–18:00, Nov–Mar, 08:00–17:00.

▼ *Below: Sumela monastery, perched perilously above a steep gorge, contains many stunning frescoes.*

Best Times to Visit

Summer is best. Even in summer it can be fairly wet, but at other times it's cool as well and the roads are prone to flooding. The mountains attract heavy snowfalls in winter.

Getting There

Domestic flights go from Istanbul to Sinop, Samsun and Trabzon. The long-distance bus journey from Istanbul is almost all by superhighway.

Getting Around

The only really sensible way to see this coast is to hire a car. The ferry which once used to run between Istanbul and Trabzon, stopping at all points en route, is no longer in operation although it may return one day. Meantime, the only public transport is by coach of which there are many, offered by a variety of companies.

Where to Stay

Samsun
Luxury
North Point Hotel, Atatürk Bulvarı 594, tel: 362 435 9595, www.northpointhotel.com Comfortable business hotel, best on offer locally.

Sinop
Mid-range
Otel 57, Meydankapı Mah. Kurtuluş Cad. 29, tel: 368 261 5462. Comfortable, basic.

Trabzon
Luxury
Zorlu Grand Hotel, Maraş Cad. 9, tel: 462 326 8400, www.zorlugrand.com Slightly tired but comfortable five-star hotel within easy distance of all the historic sights.

Safranbolu
Budget
Mehveş Hanim Konaği, Hacıhalil Mahallesi, Mescit Sok 30, tel: 370 712 8787, www.mehveshanimkonagi.com.tr One of a number of delightful restored mansions now operating as B&Bs.

Amasya
Budget
Emin Efendi Konaklari, Hatuniye Mah., Hazeranlar Sok. 66, tel: 358 213 0033, booking via www.eminefendi.com Simple, homely establishment, situated on the river bank below the Pontic tombs.

Artvin
Budget
Lapera Pansiyon, Aralık Köyü Karagöl Yolu, tel: 466 475 2125. Delightful rural guesthouse on the road between Borcka and Karagöl. Offers magnificent views and home-cooked food.

Where to Eat

Sinop
Saray Restoran, Iskele Caddesi 14, tel: 368 261 1729, no booking. Popular with the locals.

Trabzon
Fevzi Hoca Balik-Kofte, Trabzon Meydan Şubesi, K. Maraş Cad. İpekyolu İş Merkezi (Zorlu Otel Karşısı), tel: 462 326 5444. Good fish and meatballs are a speciality at this eatery. It's part of a larger chain.

Useful Contacts

Tourism Information Offices:
Artvin, Hopa Sarp Sınır Kapısı Hopa, tel: 466 371 5172.
Trabzon, Iskenderpaşa Mah. Ali Naki Efendi Sokak 1a, tel: 462 326 4760.
Safranbolu, Kaz Dağlıoğlu Maydanı 1, Safranbolu/Karabük, tel: 370 712 3863.
Turkish Airlines Offices:
Samsun, Kazimpaşa Caddesi, tel: 362 435 2330.
Trabzon, Kemer Kaya Mah., Ataturk Alani Meydan Parki Karsisi 37/A, tel: 462 321 1680. Turkish Airlines 24-hour central reservations, tel: 212 444 0849, www.thy.com.tr
Tour and Travel Agents:
Yavuztur Travel, 19 Mayis Bulvarı 35, Samsun, tel: 362 433 1770, web: www.yavuztur.com.tr

SAMSUN	J	F	M	A	M	J	J	A	S	O	N	D
AVERAGE TEMP. °F	50	51	54	59	69	74	79	80	75	69	62	55
AVERAGE TEMP. °C	10	11	12	15	19	23	26	27	24	21	17	13
RAINFALL in	3	3	3	2	2	1	1	1	2	3	3	3
RAINFALL mm	74	66	69	58	46	38	38	33	61	81	89	86
DAYS OF RAINFALL	10	10	11	9	8	6	4	4	6	7	8	9

8
Eastern Turkey

The hinterland of Eastern Turkey covers a region almost as large as that occupied by the rest of the country. If you are planning to drive from Trabzon on the Black Sea to **Van**, and then back down to the **Hatay** on the Mediterranean coast, you should allow at least a week. Double this time span if you want to visit some of the more remote sites – such as the Armenian ghost city of **Ani**, legendary **Mount Ararat**, or the curious stone heads on the 2000m (6500ft) peak of **Nemrut Dağı**.

This exotic region feels very much like the Middle East. The holy city of **Şanlıurfa** is located only 50km (30 miles) from the Syrian border. Here, modestly veiled women walk through the streets, tribesmen in Kurdish headgear abound and Arabic is spoken.

This region was also the home of Abraham (Ibrahim), the holy man who is revered by the Judaic, Christian and Muslim religions alike.

The bustling streets of ancient **Diyarbakır** have changed very little over the centuries and you will encounter water sellers and traditional scribes still noisily plying their trades (even if the latter now use the internet). For centuries Şanlıurfa and Diyarbakır traditionally looked to Damascus, Babylon and Baghdad for their trade.

Historically, Eastern Turkey has had a significant Armenian presence, and until World War I, Van remained a predominantly Armenian city within the Muslim heartland.

Don't Miss

★★★ **Nemrut Dağı:** mysterious stone heads on a remote 2000m (6500ft) peak.
★★★ **Mount Ararat:** the snow-capped mountain where Noah's Ark landed after the Flood.
★★ **Lake Van:** an inland lake almost as large as Luxembourg, with a historic city on its shore.
★★ **Ani:** spectacular remote ruins of an 11th-century Armenian city, once rival to Baghdad.
★★ **Antakya:** the ancient biblical city of Antioch.

◀ *Opposite: The Church of the Holy Cross lies on an island in Lake Van.*

Eastern Turkey

Erzurum ★

Some 300km (190 miles) southeast of Trabzon lies the remote garrison town of Erzurum. It is the highest city in Turkey and you soon become aware of the thin, cool clarity of the air which can prove both bracing and enervating.

Erzurum's strategic position has ensured that it has been overrun by all the many powers who have passed through this region, such as the Armenians, Persians, Macedonians and Romans. In the 14th century it was overrun by the Mongols, and two centuries later it fell to the Ottoman Turks under Selim the Grim.

In 1916, Erzurum fell to the Russians who had encroached on the territory since the 1877 War. A female compatriot at this time was Nenehatun, who rallied Turks

Climate

The climate in Eastern Turkey varies considerably. The Van region is **very hot** in **summer**, and **fiercely cold** in **winter**. The southern cities and the Hatay are extremely hot in summer, but pleasantly warm for the rest of the year.

to defend their city. Only later was she hailed as a seer and heroine. During this period, many houses had an outer and an inner door secured by strong locks. This was about the only defence they had against undisciplined Russian marauders. Many houses in Erzurum still have cemeteries in their back gardens and basements. During the occupation period (1916–18), nobody ventured outside the home to bury their dead in public cemeteries.

When Russians retreated in 1918, they threw sand and debris on thick patches of oil which seeped up from the ground – possibly their *raison d'être* for being in such a desolate place in the first place.

Skiers' Paradise

The Palandöken Mountains ski resort a few kilometres outside Erzurum has grown in recent years and there are now several good hotels serving four ski lifts and 22 pistes. At over 3000m there's a reasonable chance of good snow, if a fairly short season. The main runs require some experience. Après-ski is pleasant rather than wildly sophisticated. Prices are moderate and with skiers coming from Central Asia and the Middle East, the mix of people is fascinating.

KARS

Some 240km (150 miles) northeast of Erzurum is the remote, windswept city of Kars. During the 10th century it was the capital of **Armenia**, occupying the Caucasus and much of northeastern Anatolia. This was the city's golden age, though little from this era remains today other than the citadel, occupied by almost everyone at some time. In quick succession it fell to the Georgians, the Mongols and Tamerlane of Samarkand. In the 16th century the town was flattened by an earthquake.

In 1877 it was taken by the Russians (you can still see some old Czarist buildings, as well as the **Russian Orthodox Church**, now a gymnasium).

Ani ★★★

The ruins at Ani are among the most interesting and remote in the country. There has been a settlement here since the Urartian era at the beginning of the first millennium BC. The city had its golden age during the Armenian occupation, which ended in the 11th century. During this period it is said to have had a population of over 100,000 and its splendours rivalled those of Baghdad.

▼ *Below: The Yakutiye Medrese in Erzurum dates from 1310.*

▲ *Above: A boy herds goats across a landscape dominated by Mount Ararat.*
▶ *Opposite: The citadel of the ancient city of Van was built atop a dramatic promontory.*

The ruins of the walled city are entered through the **Alp Aslan Kapısı**, a Seljuk gate with a sculpture of a lion. It is the only one of the four original gates still standing. Among the ruins are the remains of several churches. Best preserved is the **Church of St Gregory the Illuminator**, erected in 1215 by the Armenian nobleman, Tigran Honentz, and dedicated to the saint who converted Armenia to Christianity in 4AD.

Some way below this church, on a ledge above the river, is the **Convent of the Virgin** (Kusanats). West of here you can see the ruins of the ancient bridge across the Ahuryan River (which now forms the border between Turkey and Armenia).

West from the Convent lies the **Cathedral**, which was started as early as 989 by Trdat Mendet. Nearby is the **Menüçehir Camii**, which is claimed to be the earliest Seljuk mosque in Turkey. It has a lovely mosaic ceiling, as well as a stub minaret which affords a good view of the ruins.

The Lost Ark?

The biblical story of Noah's Ark landing on Mount Ararat after the Flood was usually accepted as a myth. Then in 1951, an expedition ascending the mountain came across several spars of ancient wood high up, preserved in the permanent ice. These looked curiously like the superstructure of a large boat. Photographs were taken of the exciting find, but subsequent expeditions have been unable to locate the exact spot where the wood was seen. It is thought to have been reburied by snowfalls. Increasing global warming, however, has renewed hopes that the intriguing discovery may once again reappear.

MOUNT ARARAT

Known in Turkish as Ağrı Dağı, this mountain lies at the easternmost extremity of Turkey, some 320km (200 miles) east of Erzurum. Its permanently snow-capped peak rises to 5183m (16,853ft), and the mountain itself straddles the borders of Turkey, Iran and Armenia.

According to the Old Testament of the Bible, this is where **Noah's Ark** first made landfall after the Flood. The perfectly cone-shaped mountain forms a spectacular backdrop to the remote, flat plain, and nearby towards the Iranian border there is a large meteor crater.

For treks up Mount Ararat, *see* At a Glance, page 121. Application must be made at least three months beforehand. The last stages of the arduous climb usually require oxygen, and the hike is not recommended for inexperienced climbers.

LAKE VAN

This vast inland lake lies 320km (200 miles) southeast of Erzurum. As it has no outlet, the only loss of water occurs through evaporation, which has left the water saturated with such a **highly alkaline** concentration of mineral salts, that you can wash your clothes here without using soap. A word of warning: it's safe to swim in the lake, but the sodium will painfully sting any open wound.

Akdamar Adası ★★★

This island in the southeast corner of Lake Van is reached by regular ferry from the mainland quay just opposite. It is the site of the 10th-century **Church of the Holy Cross**, one of the most exquisite Armenian churches in existence. The detailed reliefs covering the outside walls of the church depict scenes from the Bible, including a doglike whale with ears, swallowing Jonah.

Van Cats

The Van region is home to the famous Van cats. These cats have distinctive white fur, and eyes of different colours. They are said to enjoy swimming in the waters of Lake Van, where they hunt for *darekh* (a rare form of carp), which has adapted to survive in the sodium-saturated waters. Legend has it that the Van cats originally arrived from India by way of the Silk Route. They may, in fact, have been brought to Anatolia by the first gypsies, who worked as metal-beaters repairing the shields and armour of invading armies.

Van ★★★

This historic town lies on the eastern shore of Lake Van, about 100km (65 miles) from the Iranian border. The citadel of the ruined ancient city is on a promontory above the lake, known as the **Rock of Van**. This can be reached by regular dolmuş service from the town centre, 4km (2½ miles) to the east. The Hittites had a settlement here as early as the 13th century BC. On the north side of the rock is the tomb of a Muslim saint, which attracts pilgrims from far and wide. Above this is a rare and ancient Urartian temple, one of only a few discovered so far. At the top of the Citadel are the remains of an ancient castle and several mosques. Below the rock, to the south, you can see the silent ruins of Old Van, which was destroyed in 1915 during a struggle for an Armenian republic in Eastern Turkey.

A Word of Warning

For all its splendid history and scenery, much of the southeast region has been a Kurdish stronghold and clashes with the Turkish army have been frequent. After several years of welcome ceasefire, Kurdish separatists have now renewed their campaign of violence and have been targeting tourist destinations. Anyone planning to travel in the region should take local advice before going and be aware of their security at all times. In view of the current unrest in neighbouring states, it is recommended that visitors should not travel within 10km (6 miles) of the Syrian/Iraqi borders.

The Van Museum north of the modern town centre has some fascinating Urartian gold ornaments, as well as figurines dating from this mysterious period. The upstairs section of the museum contains a display of skulls and bones related to the Armenian struggle for autonomy.

THE SOUTH

Diyarbakır ★★

This is the ancient capital of upper **Mesopotamia**, which for centuries attracted Syrian, Persian, Babylonian and Kurdish traders. Some archaeologists believe that it may well be the oldest continuously inhabited city in the world. Remains dating back from as long ago as the Stone Age have been found on this site.

The ancient city centre is surrounded by walls that still have over 60 of their original 72 towers intact. The **Ulu Camii** (Great Mosque) is over 900 years old, and incorporates the remains of a 7th-century Christian church. The 16th-century **Safa Camii** is built in the distinctive Persian style, and near the east gate there is even an old **Surp Giragos Kilisesi** (Armenian Church).

Diyarbakır professes to be the 'World's Watermelon Capital' and each year at the end of September holds a festival to celebrate this claim to fame. The high point is the judging of the largest watermelon. Winning entries sometimes exceed a massive 50kg (110 pounds).

Şanlıurfa

Travelling 180km (110 miles) southwest of Diyarbakır, you reach Şanlıurfa (Glorious Urfa), a city of biblical antiquity and religious importance.

Just south of the city centre lies **Abraham's Cave**, where, according to a legend sacred to Christians, Jews and Muslims, Abraham was born. It is said that Abraham sheltered here for the first 10 years of his life, evading **King Nimrod's** decree that all local children be put to death. Years later Abraham was captured by Nimrod, who ordered him to be burnt at the stake, but Jehovah made a spring gush from the ground which extinguished the fire. Nearby you can see the pools which are filled by this spring. The carp who live in it are said to be centuries old.

In the Citadel are the two ancient columns known as the **Throne of Nimrod**, and nearby is a Crusader castle whose ruins provide fine views over the city's old quarter. The bazaar is one of the most oriental in all Turkey.

▲ *Above: Mysterious stone heads line the peak of Nemrut Dağı.*
◀ *Opposite: Locals admire the sacred pools at Şanlıurfa.*

South of Şanlıurfa, ancient Harran is famous for its **beehive houses**, and as home of the **Temple of Sin** and the first **Islamic University**.

Just north of Şanlıurfa, the **GAP Project** is a vast scheme to harness the waters of the Tigris and Euphrates rivers, with a staggering network of 22 dams, 19 hydro-electric plants and hundreds of kilometres of irrigation tunnels and canals. The Atatürk Dam alone is the fourth largest in the world. It is transforming the economy of the region but is less well received by Turkey's Middle Eastern neighbours – Iran, Iraq and Syria, who also depend on the rivers, and by Kurdish separatists who claim this land for an independent Kurdistan.

Nemrut Dağı ★★★

Mount Nemrut stands 2000m (6500ft) high in a remote region near Adıyaman. The area is scattered with **stone heads** and relief panels. There are two rows of statues carved from 5-tonne stone blocks, each over 8m (26ft) high. The statues were the work of **King Antiochus** who ruled the Commagene Kingdom from 160BC to AD72. Today we might deem this a sect but the giant torsos represent the pagan gods Antiochus worshipped and whom he believed bestowed divine powers on him.

The First Horoscope

At Nemrut Dağı, a unique sandstone panel shows a life-size lion, along with stars, a crescent moon and planets. Historians and astronomers are convinced that their configuration commemorates the moment of King Antiochus' coronation. By modern calendars, this would be 14 July 109BC, which would make it the oldest known horoscope in history.

▲ *Above: Once a city of great wealth, Antakya retains a good deal of character.*

The heads have long since become detached from the giant bodies and were all but unknown until Karl Puchstein, a German engineer, discovered them in 1881. They have perplexed and fascinated scholars, but recently a Dutch-German scientific team has located Antiochus' **burial chamber** hidden in the mountainside. Excavations have begun and it is hoped the tomb may yield riches and treasures comparable to the tomb of the Egyptian pharaoh, Tutankhamen. Few rulers in history took such elaborate pains to build a commemorative tomb in such an utterly remote site. Most visitors try to reach the top before sunrise to catch the fabulous views.

HATAY

This finger of land runs south along the coast and juts into **Syria**. The Hatay became part of Turkey as late as 1939, and many of its inhabitants still speak Arabic. Prior to 1939 this region had been ruled by the French, who used it as a secret diplomatic bargaining tool to keep Turkey out of World War II. A local referendum was held, and the inhabitants voted to become part of Turkey. The French handed over the Hatay, thereby ensuring Turkey's neutrality throughout the war. Doubts have since been cast upon the result of this plebiscite, which in turn have given rise to occasional unrest in Antakya, the main city of the Hatay.

Karatepe ★★

One of the finest and most accessible Hittite sites, Karatepe's walls and gates are covered with splendid storybook tellings of the exploits of the local kings and other grand statuary. It was here that archaeologists finally managed to decipher Hittite hieroglyphics.

Antakya ★★

Antakya (ancient **Antioch**), 320km (200 miles) southwest of Şanlıurfa, was founded in the 4th century BC by one of Alexander the Great's generals, **Seleucos Nicator**. Within two centuries Antioch had become one of the greatest

Pillar Sitting

This early Christian craze was started by **St Simeon Stylites** in the 4th century. He was soon copied by Simeon the Younger, a misanthropic anchorite spent a quarter of a century perched on his pillar near Antioch (Antakya), contemplating the evils of the world below. Occasionally he would deliver fiery sermons to the assembled populace. He was by no means the only one to join the craze – at one time there were over 250 of these eccentrics occupying the moral high ground.

cities in the world. It gained much of its wealth from being the main port at the Mediterranean end of the Silk Route, which brought caravans loaded with spices and rare goods from Asia. During Roman times Antioch, the third city of the Empire after Rome and Alexandria, gained a reputation for notoriously licentious behaviour, which attracted people from far and wide. Among these were a number of early Christians, determined to put a stop to all the debauchery (*see* panel, page 118).

Sen Piyer Kilisesi ★★

In a cave near Antioch, Sts Peter, Paul and Barnabas officially created the Christian church before setting out to evangelize across the Roman Empire. Miraculously the cave church still exists, complete with the escape hatch used by early Christians who worshipped in fear of their lives as Christianity was banned at the time. Mosaics on the floor date from AD500; the façade was added by the Crusaders. Open 08:00–12:00 and 13:30–17:30 Tue–Sun.

Hatay Museum ★★

The other main sight in Antakya is the Hatay Museum, which houses one of the world's best collections of **Roman mosaics**, preserved much as they must have been 2000 years ago. Some depict mythological scenes, others show scenes from everyday Roman life, giving us an insight into what the Ancient Romans must have been like as people. Open Tue–Sun Apr–Oct 09:00–18:30, Nov–Mar 09:00–17:30.

Harbiye ★★

The **resort** of Harbiye can be reached by regular dolmuş from the city bus station. Since earliest times (when it was known as Daphne) this has been a popular spot with locals fleeing the heat of the city. The attractions at Harbiye include a **waterfall** and a **cool leafy valley** with pools and tinkling water among the popular tea houses.

HARBIYE

Named after Daphne, who turned herself into a grove of laurel trees to escape from Apollo, what is now Harbiye was a trendy Roman holiday resort, used by Anthony and Cleopatra for their Egyptian-style wedding in 40BC. Most of the mosaics in the Hatay museum come from wealthy villas in the area.

▼ *Below:* Orpheus Charming the Beasts *in Antakya's Archaeological Museum.*

Best Times to Visit

Although the climate varies from region to region in Eastern Turkey, it invariably gets very hot during summer. Winters are crippling and there are frequent snowstorms. Erzurum has temperatures well below zero for most of the winter. May and September are ideal months to visit but, if you are a skier, the Palandöken resorts have thick snow from November through until March.

Getting There

There are regular domestic flights from Istanbul and Ankara to all the main cities in this region. Erzurum or Van can be reached by rail. If you're a train buff, you'll love it. If not, it is a long (two-day) journey. The bus journey from Istanbul or Ankara can be an 18 or 20 hour marathon but this is the most comfortable and economical way to go.

Getting Around

The most convenient way to get around in this region is by car, especially if you want to visit some of the more remote sights. The main roads are generally tarred and perfectly driveable in an ordinary saloon car. The same applies to the road to Ani, although the road to Nemrut Dağı is merely a track in certain places. One of the best journeys in this region is to go by ferry from the town of Van to Tatvan which lies over 100km (65 miles) to the west across the oily-calm waters of Lake Van. You can then take the bus back around the southern shores of the lake, past Akdamar Island.

Where to Stay

Antakya (Hatay)

Mid-range

Savon Hotel, Kurtulus Caddesi 192, tel: 326 214 6355, fax: 326 214 6356, www.savonhotel.com.tr A stone-built Ottoman soap and olive oil factory charmingly and originally restored, with a good Turkish-Italian restaurant.

The Liwan Hotel, Gullubahce Mah. Silahli Kuvvetler Cad. No 5, tel: 326 215 7777, www.theliwanhotel.com An extravagant 1920s town centre mansion transformed into a small, traditionally furnished boutique hotel, and wonderfully located within walking distance of most sights. Restaurant, bar and café.

Diyarbakır

Mid-range

Otel Büyük Kervansaray, Gazi Caddesi, Deliller Hanı, Mardinkapı, tel: 412 228 9606. With every room different, a fabulous courtyard, small pool, restaurant and *hamam*, this restored caravansaray may not be the most up-market hotel in town, but it is certainly the most entertaining.

Erzurum

Luxury

Dedeman Palandöken Ski Centre, tel: 442 317 0500, www.dedeman.com/SkiLodge.aspx One of a growing number of excellent ski hotels in the mountains, convenient for the pistes.

Kâhta

Budget

New Kommagene Hotel, Yavuz Selim Mahellesi M. Kemal Cad. No 3, Adiyaman, Kâhta 02400, tel: 416 725 9726, www.kommagenehotel.com Good, cheap, clean and cheerful hotel with parking and English-speaking staff. Camping possible.

Şanlıurfa

Mid-range

Hilton Garden Inn, Karakoyunlu Mah 11 Nisan Fuar Cad, Şanlıurfa 63100, tel: 414 318 5000, http://hiltongardeninn.hilton.co.uk International 4-star gloss arrives with the Hilton chain. Plenty of comfort and relatively little individuality. About 15 mins' walk from the sights.

Hotel Harran, Atatürk Bulvarı, tel: 414 313 2860, www.hotelharran.com Considered to be the best hotel in town.

Hotel El-Ruha, Balıklıgöl Yanı Lekeler Caddesi, tel: 414 215 4411, www.hotelelruha.com Faded grandeur across from the pools of Abraham. Own pool, fine restaurant, castle views. No alcohol.

Harran Evi, Harran Evi Ibni Teymiye Mahallesi, Harran, tel: 542 337 8512 or 544 254 7983, www.harrankulturevi.net Spend a night in restored beehive mudhuts in the ancient village of Harran.

Van

MID-RANGE

Merit Şahmaran, Yeniköy Mevkii 12km, 65170 Edremit, Van, tel: 432 312 3060, www.meritsahmaranotel.com Comfortable 4-star on the edge of the lake 12km from city centre.

Gaziantep

Anadolu Evleri, Şekeroğlu Mahellesi Köroğlu Sokak 6, Şahinbey, tel: 342 220 9525, www.anadoluevleri.com Four beautifully restored city centre courtyard houses, filled with antiques. Every room is different so standards vary wildly.

WHERE TO EAT

Antakya

Hatay Sultan Sofrası, İstiklâl Caddesi 20A. Antakya, tel: 236 213 8759, www.sultansofrasi.com Large, cheap and cheerful local serving excellent *pide*, kebabs and baklava.

Sveyka, Kurtulus Caddesi 58, tel: 326 213 3947, www.sveyka.com Traditional local specialities served with a flourish in a grand old historic mansion slightly off the main drag.

Gaziantep

Şirvan Baklava, İncilipınar Mahallersi Ali Fuat Cebesoy Bulvası (Grand Otel Karşısı) Şehitkamil/Gaziantep, tel: 342 324 2526, www.sirvanusta.com A simple menu, but worth it – kebabs, lahmacun, but above all, fabulous baklava created by a master craftsman.

Diyarbakır

The best restaurants are in the best hotels. There are plenty of small restaurants inside the city walls, along Inönü and Izzet Paşa Caddesi, and small fish restaurants near Hazar Lake.

Selim Amcanın Sofra Salonu, Ali Emiri Cad. No 22, tel: 412 224 4447, Diyarbakır, www.kaburgaciselimamca.com Rather spartan, but the food is excellent (barbecue and nomadic options).

Erzurum

Güzelyurt Restoran, Cumhuriyet Caddesi, tel: 442 234 5001, www.guzelyurtrestaurant.com.tr Open since 1922, this is about the only up-market non-hotel restaurant in town, all soft lighting and soft music.

Erzurum Evleri, Cumhuriyet Caddesi, Yüzbaşı Sokak, tel: 442 213 8372, www.erzurumevleri.com Stunning traditional inn; lounge around on cushions, smoking a *nargile* and eating local dishes.

Şanlıurfa

Çevahir Konuk Evi, Büyükyol Selahattin Eyyubi Camii Karşısı, tel: 414 215 9377, www.cevahirkonukevi.com Elegant restaurant, serving fabulous food in traditional style. Also has rooms.

Van

Breakfast is a big thing in Van with a whole street, Kahvalticilar Sokak (literally Breakfast St) lined by breakfast restaurants offering an assortment of hot and cold dishes. Join in.

TOURS AND EXCURSIONS

Treks to climb **Mount Ararat** are organized by:

Middle Earth Travel, Gaferli Mah Cevizler Sokak 20, 50180 Göreme, tel: 384 271 2559, www.middleearthtravel.com

Excursions to **Nemrut Dağı** are offered by several companies in Şanlıurfa. Trips to **Ani** can be arranged through the **Tourist Information Office** in Kars.

USEFUL CONTACTS

Tourist Information Offices:

Diyarbakır, Dağkapı Burcu Giriş Bölümü, tel: 412 221 2173.

Bitlis, Kültür Merkezi Binası, Tatvan, tel. 434 827 6300.

Kars, Cumhuriyet Mahallesi Lise Sok. 15, tel: 474 212 6865, 212 6864 or 212 6817.

Antakya, Şehit Mustafa Sevgi Caddesi 8/A, Müdür, tel: 326 214 9217 or 216 0610.

Iskenderun, Atatürk Bulvarı 49, tel: 326 614 1620.

Turkish Airlines: www.thy.com.tr

24-hour central reservations tel: 212 444 0849.

KARS	J	F	M	A	M	J	J	A	S	O	N	D
AVERAGE TEMP. °F	21	25	34	50	63	70	77	79	71	59	44	29
AVERAGE TEMP. °C	-6	-4	1	10	17	21	25	26	22	15	7	-2
RAINFALL in	1	1	1	2	3	3	2	2	1	2	1	1
RAINFALL mm	28	28	28	43	86	74	53	53	31	41	31	25
DAYS OF RAINFALL	7	7	8	9	15	12	8	7	5	7	6	7

Travel Tips

Tourist Information

www.goturkey.com

Main overseas offices:

UK: Fourth floor, 29-30 St James' Street, London SW1A 1HB, tel: 020 7839 7778/4 web: www.gototurkey.co.uk

USA: 821 United Nations Plaza, New York NY 10017, tel: 212 687 2169; 5055 Wilshire Boulevard, Los Angeles, CA 90036, tel: 323 937 8066, web: www.tourismturkey.org

Germany: Baselerstr. 35-37/1, 60329 Frankfurt, tel: 49 6923 3081/2, e-mail: info@reiseland-tuerkei-info.de website: www.reiseland-tuerkei-info.de

Netherlands: Turkish Culture and Tourism Office, Turkish Embassy Information Counsellor's Office, Hofweg 1C-2511 AA, The Hague, tel: 31 70 346 9998, 346 7767, fax: 31 70 364 4468, e-mail: ttoinfo@planet.nl web: www.welkominturkije.nl

Sweden: Kungsgaten 3, 5-111 43 Stockholm, tel: 46 8 679 8320/1, e-mail: info@tourism.turkemb.se web: www.turism.turkemb.se

Denmark: Vesterbrogade 11A, 1620 Copenhagen V, tel: 45 31 22 3100 and 22 8374, e-mail: turkishtourism@mail.tele.dk www.tyrkietturisme.dk

Entry Requirements

Everyone needs a valid passport to enter Turkey for a stay of 90 days or less. Citizens of Australia, Canada, and New Zealand do not need a visa. Citizens of the USA, Ireland and the UK require a visa, obtainable at the point of entry (hard currency only; more expensive if obtained in advance). Most other countries require a visa and should get one ahead of travelling. Check before departure for up-to-date regulations (www.mfa.gov.tr). For stays in excess of the allotted three-month period, a **residence permit** (*ikâmet tezkeresi*) is required, as well as documented proof that you are able to support yourself. You must apply at a Turkish Consulate in your country of residence and allow time for lengthy paperwork. Working at almost any job, even shoe shining, is not permitted for non-Turks. If you are sent by your company to work, you will need a **work permit**.

Customs

Entry into Turkey is comparatively easy. There are a few nominal limits on **duty-free** goods, mainly: 200 cigarettes, 50 cigars, and 200g tobacco (you may buy an additional 400 cigarettes and 100 cigars at duty free on arrival), 1.5kg coffee, 1.5kg instant coffee, 500g tea, 1kg chocolate and 1kg sweets, and 5 litres of wine or spirits. High-value items may be listed in your passport and must accompany you when you leave. If you arrive by road, customs will record your vehicle in your passport. As elsewhere, heavy penalties are in force for carrying or possession of **illegal substances** or **weapons**, either into or out of Turkey. On exiting Turkey, your passport will also be stamped. If you have bought items like carpets or valuable jewellery, ensure your vendor provides a **purchase certificate**, at the time of sale, showing it is not **antique** – over 100 years old.

Health Requirements

Turkey requires no health certificates on entry. However, you are advised to keep your tetanus and typhoid jabs up to date. Most foreign clinics strongly recommend you to be vaccinated against hepatitis B before arriving in Turkey.

Getting There

By Air: There are regular scheduled international flights to Ankara and Istanbul (International), Izmir and Antalya with national carrier Turkish Airlines, British Airlines and many others. A variety of low-cost airlines including easyJet and Pegasus fly into Istanbul

Sabiha Gokçen and airports around the coast, and Pegasus and other low-cost domestic airlines offer a wide network of internal connections throughout the country. In summer there are also many charter services to tourist resorts.

By Train: International train services connect from Europe via Bulgaria and Greece and on to Asia (Iran and Iraq) via Van. Services to Syria via Gaziantep are currently disrupted. Interrail cards are valid in Turkey. www.tcdd.gov.tr

By Ferry: There are regular ferry services between Greece and Turkey, the main ones being those between Chios and Çesme, Samos and Kuşadası, Rhodes and Marmaris.

By Road: You can travel overland from Bulgaria and Greece.

What to Pack

In spring and autumn, evenings can be cool and damp. Bring a cardigan or jacket. Summers have become somewhat hotter and the coastal areas oppressively humid. At resorts, dress is casual and shorts, beachwear or flimsy dresses are fine on the beach, although a little more discretion in town is polite. In more reverent cities, like Bursa or Konya, and in all mosques modest clothes are appropriate; cover knees and shoulders. All resorts sell beachwear, watersport gear and suncreams, usually cheaper than you will find at home. Warm clothes will be needed if travelling in winter or in the mountains.

Money Matters

Currency: The Turkish lira (TL) is divided into 100 kuruş. There are 10, 25 and 50 kuruş and 1TL coins, and 5, 10, 20, 50 and 100TL notes. Most traders are happy to deal in Euros, US dollars or GB pounds, but you may find the prices better if you trade in TL.

Exchange: Banking hours are 08:30–noon, 13:30–17:00 Monday–Friday. In the resorts they sometimes stay open later in the evening. Foreign money can also be changed to Turkish Lira (TL) at post offices (PTT), and change boutiques (*Döviz Para*) which usually give a better rate than banks and charge no commission for buying foreign notes. Travellers' cheques are all but obsolete these days. Credit cards are accepted almost everywhere, but many places do not accept American Express and you may be asked to pay a premium if using a card; 24-hour automatic teller machines (ATMs) are found even in the smallest places. Machines take most recognized credit and personal bankers cards. You need your PIN number. ATMs usually dispense a maximum of about 300 TL per card per day. Bank staff will help you if you want to withdraw more than this.

Tipping: In most restaurants 10–15% is added to your bill. With taxis, round up your fare. VAT of 18% is always included in retail purchases. The tipping of Turkish bath attendants is customary.

Accommodation

Accommodation in Turkey is less expensive than many other places. If you come in an organized tour group, even luxury accommodation is good value. The top end of the market is very luxurious indeed, and the bottom end tends to be pensions. Bargaining is acceptable at both ends of the scale. On the south or Aegean coast, it is worth paying a small premium for air conditioning. In winter check heating and hot water; many places use solar heating and the water can be freezing.

Public Holidays

1 January • New Year's Day
23 April • National Independence and Children's Day
19 May • Atatürk Commemoration and Youth and Sports
30 August • Victory Day
29 October • Republic Day
Moveable holidays: Ramazan (month-long fast)
Şeker Bayram (sugar festival at the end of Ramazan)
Kurban Bayram (Feast of Sacrifice, 20 days after the end of Ramazan)

Eating Out

Turkey has different types of restaurant. Top of the list is the **restoran**. The best in Istanbul and Ankara are comparable to establishments found in any major metropolis. The ones which specialize in Ottoman cuisine (i.e. food consumed by the sultans) provide a superb culinary experience. Lesser restorans such as those in the resorts will often have a fair range of international cuisine. Next is the **lokanta**, cheap, cheerful and plentiful. Here you'll get authentic local cuisine at reasonable prices, often served in a cafeteria setting. The range of choice is much wider than you'd expect. Lowest on the scale, but good nevertheless, is the **kebabci**, serving a large *kebap* on a revolving skewer (doner) or grilled cubes of meat (*şiş*). *Kebap* with salad and yoghurt, in a piece of pitta bread, can make a filling snack or an inexpensive meal. The **pideci** serves the Turkish equivalent of pizza, baked in an oven, while *börek* (stuffed pastry) is another good cheap snack.

Transport

Air: Turkish Airlines (www.thy.com) has an extensive internal flight network. It also flies to many major world capitals. Low cost carriers Pegasus Air (www.flypgs.com) and Onur Air (www.onurair.com.tr) also offer a wide range of domestic flights.
Buses: Most major cities have modern bus terminals and service is akin to air travel with on-board videos, snacks, air conditioning and comfortable seats. Companies like Varan, Kâmil Koç and Ulusoy have good safety records and run scheduled routes to major destinations. Booking is advisable; this is probably done most easily through a travel agent as each company runs a separate kiosk and there is no central booking desk or timetable at the bus station to allow you to compare prices and timings. Smoking is forbidden.
Car Hire: This is pricey by any standards. Car hire is more regulated of late and even smaller operators must maintain safe fleets of late-model cars. Jeep Safaris are popular. All major rental agencies operate in Turkey but you can make substantial savings on a Fly-Drive scheme, paying in your own currency before you leave. Turkey also has some of the most expensive fuel in the world, so go for a fuel-efficient vehicle. Diesel is noticeably cheaper than petrol. Insurance4carhire.com (tel: +44 (0) 1242 538 475) is a cheap British annual scheme which will ensure your CDW.
Driving: Turkey has splendid motorway systems linking major cities. Many visitors shun driving due to dire warnings and Turkey's unrivalled accident rate. Turkish drivers have a spirit of adventure but lack driving skills or road sense. At night, vehicles are often unlit. You'll need all your skill and a bit of nerve as well, but being independent has its rewards. Bring your local driving license, and, if bringing your own car, a Green Card covering you for insurance. If you are in an accident, don't move your car or let anyone else do so until the police arrive.
Taxis: Taxis throughout Turkey are relatively cheap and, unless it rains, there are swarms of them. In big cities, with the large influx of migrant workers, taxi driving is a popular profession. Most are honest, but it helps to have your address written down on a piece of paper and get some idea of what the price should be. Check if they are going to use the meter, and if they insist on a fixed fare, agree the fare before getting in. Airport taxis are usually on a set rate.
Dolmuş: This minibus service covers most of the shorter bus routes and inner cities. It's a bit more expensive than a bus, but more friendly and often more convenient. The minibus leaves as soon as it is full, and the driver will drop you off anywhere along the route.
Ferries: Ferries, often taking vehicles, go from Istanbul to Izmir and Bodrum, Bursa (Yalova), the Sea of Marmara Island, the Princes' Islands and

Conversion Chart

From	To	Multiply By
Millimetres	Inches	0.0394
Metres	Yards	1.0936
Metres	Feet	3.281
Kilometres	Miles	0.6214
Square kilometres	Square miles	0.386
Hectares	Acres	2.471
Litres	Pints	1.760
Kilograms	Pounds	2.205
Tonnes	Tons	0.984

To convert Celsius to Fahrenheit: x 9 ÷ 5 + 32

the Black Sea. Routes from Brindisi and Venice in Italy connect with Çeşme near Izmir, while there are services across to northern Cyprus from several cities on the Mediterranean coast including Mersin and Alanya. Between Bodrum and the Greek island of Kos and from Bodrum to Datça, services run twice a day in the summer. In winter, most services continue but less frequently. Details are best obtained from local tourism information offices. Useful sources of information for advanced planning include two websites: www.feribot.net (run by Anker Travel, Kuşadası, tel: 256 612 4598), and http://ferries-turkey.com (run by Aegaean Tour Travel, tel: +90 (0)252 313 0722). Both offer online booking for a variety of domestic and international ferry services.
Trains: There's a somewhat sparse but useful network of rail routes fanning out across Turkey including the most heavily used sleeper service between Istanbul and Ankara, a useful route roughly following the Aegean coast, and connections to the far east of the country. Major works are currently upgrading key lines to high-speed services and the long-delayed Marmaray project in Istanbul will connect Europe and Asia by rail. The trains are excellent value but heavily booked by locals. Details and bookings from TCDD, Haydarpaşa Station, tel: 216 348 8020 or Ankara, tel: 312 311 0620, website: www.tcdd.gov.tr

USEFUL PHRASES

Günaydın • Good day
Afiyet olsun • enjoy your meal/drink (bon appetit)
Ne kadar? • How much is it?
Şerefe! • Cheers!
Tuvalet var mı? • Is there a toilet here?
Bir dakika (bir daka) • Wait a minute
Boş ver • Let it go, forget it
Saat kaç? • What time is it?
Gidelim mi? • Shall we go?
Inşallah • Hopefully, God willing
Maalesef • Regrettably, there isn't any
Sakın ol • Keep calm
Tamam mı? • Agreed? OK?

Business Hours

Many establishments close for lunch, especially government offices and banks. Normal working hours are 09:00–12:00 and 13:00–17:00, or 09:00–12:30 and 13:30–17:30. In resort areas, post offices don't close for lunch and are often open late in the evening. From May to October, tourism information offices are open 7 days a week. Museums that close on Mondays in winter are often open 7 days a week in summer but there are no firm rules. Check before you set out.

Time Difference

Turkey is two hours ahead of Greenwich Mean (or Universal Standard) Time (GMT). Turkey operates summer time (GMT +3) between late Mar and Oct.

Communications

Most public telephones use telephone cards in prepaid units. Large post offices have plenty of phone booths, or look for a sign that says, 'Kontur Telefon'. After you call, you pay in cash according to units used. Increasingly, public telephones accept credit cards. Many people now have mobile, GSM, telephones and they are as much a status symbol in Turkey as elsewhere.

Electricity

220 volts, 50 AC. Plugs are two-pronged, but there are two different sizes. One rarely encounters difficulties and any appliance that works in Europe will work in Turkey. Voltage can be very low in some areas.

Weights and Measures

Turkey uses the metric system.

Health Precautions

If you are visiting eastern provinces in Turkey, malaria is still found and you should bring appropriate medicines. Polio is prevalent in rural areas and, if you are trekking or hiking off the beaten track, dogs may carry **rabies**. Most international brand-name medications and drugs are available from all pharmacies along with Turkish-produced generic brands. Many pharmacies now stock injectable medicines in a steripack with its own syringe. Excepting addictive drugs, all medicines and antibiotics are available over the counter without a doctor's prescription. Should you need to go to a doctor or to **hospital**, many state-of-the-art private hospitals and clinics have foreign-trained profes-

Media

International magazines and newspapers are available the day after publication in main cities through DÜNYA shops. Resort areas have a selection of pulp press in the high season. The Ankara-based Turkish Daily News (TDN) is published daily in English and takes a relatively unbiased stand on many Turkish issues. Satellite TV means you probably won't miss much of what is going on at home either.

sionals. You have to pay first (most accept credit cards) but ensure your holiday insurance covers reimbursement for private medical treatment. Many experience **diarrhoea** due to the richer diet; eating and drinking sensibly for the first few days is a good precaution. Drink bottled **water** and, in extreme heat, add salt to your diet and go at a slower pace.

Personal Safety

Turkey has a good, if not exceptional record for personal safety. Male chauvinism is still very much alive and whether they want it or not, single women will attract attention. Generally, if you are dressed appropriately, the attention will be respectful. In the resort areas, where the locals are becoming increasingly used to Western habits, men may be more persistent. If in doubt, shout and you will be rescued. The resorts tend to have their disco alleys, where tourist drunks are the main hazard. Use common sense.

Emergencies

Ambulance, tel: 112
Fire Brigade, tel: 110.
Police, tel: 155 (this number for emergencies only).
Traffic Police (Alo Trafik), tel: 154.
Other useful numbers are:
Gendarmerie, tel: 156.
International Telephone Operator (for reverse charge calls), tel: 115.
Directory Enquiries, tel: 118.
Wake-up Call, tel: 135.

Best Buys

Turkish carpets and kilims are world-renowned. Fashions and leather garments are good buys and excellent quality. In Istanbul, go to Zeytinburnu where leather wholesalers are concentrated. You can buy retail from all shops here and bargains are to be had. All the global brand-name fashions are found in large cities at good prices. Jeans represent excellent value and many are made in Turkey. Leather accessories like bags, brief cases and shoes are good value. Names to look for: Tergan and Desa. Men's dress and casual shirts in top quality poplin are a steal and so are silk ties. Bisse is one of the top names. Gold jewellery is excellent value – this doesn't mean cheap trinkets or 'village girl' gold bangles! Spices and ceramics make good gifts to take home.

Good Reading

- Goodwin, Jason (2007) *The Janissary Tree* (and other Yashim the Eunuch novels).
- Kemal, Yaşar (1990) *Mehmet My Hawk*. Collins.
- Lord Kinross (1990) *Atatürk, the Rebirth of a Nation*. Weidenfeld.
- Loti, Pierre (1989) *Aziyade*. KPI Paperbacks.
- Macaulay, Rose (1990) *The Towers of Trebizond*. Flamingo.
- Morris, Chris (2006) *The New Turkey: The Quiet Revolution on the Edge of Europe.*
- Norwich, John Julius (1995) *Byzantium, the Decline and Fall.* Viking.
- Anything by Orhan Pamuk.
- Seal, Jeremy (1996) *A Fez of the Heart*, (2012) *Meander.*

Numbers

One • *Bir*
Two • *Iki*
Three • *Üç*
Four • *Dört*
Five • *Beş*
Six • *Altı*
Seven • *Yedi*
Eight • *Sekiz*
Nine • *Dokuz*
10 • *On*
11 • *On bir*
12 • *On iki*
20 • *Yirmi*
30 • *Otuz*
40 • *Kırk*
50 • *Elli*
60 • *Altmış*
70 • *Yetmiş*
80 • *Seksen*
90 • *Doksan*
100 • *Yüz*
110 • *Yüz on*
200 • *Iki yüz*
300 • *Üç yüz*
1000 • *Bin*
2000 • *Iki Bin*
1,000,000 • *Bir milyon*

INDEX

Note: Numbers in **bold** indicate photographs

INDEX